DR. TOM MALONE

PREACHES ON

THE APOSTLES

DR. TOM MALONE

P R E A C H E S   O N

THE APOSTLES

SWORD of the LORD
PUBLISHERS
P. O. BOX 1099, MURFREESBORO, TN 37133

Introduction

THE TWELVE IN THE GOSPELS

Matthew 10:2-4	Mark 3:16-19	Luke 6:13-16
1. Simon Peter	Simon Peter	Simon Peter
2. Andrew	James	Andrew
3. James	John	James
4. John	Andrew	John
5. Philip	Philip	Philip
6. Bartholomew	Bartholomew	Bartholomew
7. Thomas	Matthew	Matthew
8. Matthew	Thomas	Thomas
9. James	James	James
10. Lebbaeus	Thaddaeus	Simon
11. Simon	Simon	Judas
12. Judas Iscariot	Judas Iscariot	Judas Iscariot

In these three listings, Simon Peter is always mentioned first and Judas Iscariot last.

THE TWELVE IN ACTS
Acts 1:13, 14, 26

Peter	Bartholomew
James	Matthew
John	James (Son of Alphaeus)
Andrew	Simon (Zelotes)
Philip	Judas (Brother of James)
Thomas	Matthias (Elected to take the place of Judas Iscariot)

In this listing, Judas Iscariot is not mentioned at all. Acts 1:25 explains why. Matthias is chosen in his place (Acts 1:26) and is never mentioned again, except collectively.

Some, such as A. B. Bruce, divide the twelve into three groups of four. The two sets of brothers, Peter and Andrew, then James and his brother, John, supposedly form the first group of four and are the best known. Philip, Nathanael, Thomas, and Matthew form the second group of four and are less known than the first group. James (son of Alphaeus), Lebbaeus, Simon and Judas Iscariot form the third group of four and supposedly are the least known.

In the first place, such grouping is not significant and provides no worthy consideration of the twelve. The proposed grouping breaks down when we consult the gospels and their records. Jesus chose three disciples, Peter, James and John, to accompany Him to the Mount of Transfiguration and to the raising of the young dead girl. He took these three deeper into the bloody Garden of Gethsemane than any of the others. The third grouping of four, supposedly the least known, had one of the best known in the grouping, namely, Judas Iscariot. He was known for his infamy, yet well known.

In his famous painting of the Last Supper, Leonardo da Vinci seems to have grouped the disciples in clusters of threes. Perhaps because of Bible truth that there was at least one group of three: Peter, James and John.

What is more significant than any systematic divisions of the twelve is the number "twelve" itself. Jesus could have chosen ten or twenty. Why twelve? Twelve is a most significant number in the Bible. It is said to be the number which represents governmental perfection and rule.

There were twelve patriarchs, sons of Israel, apostles, gates and foundations. Jesus made His first public appearance, since His birth, at the age of twelve. Twelve is an important number in the Bible and there is a definite reason why Christ chose twelve disciples rather than some other number. When Peter asked the Lord, "Behold we have forsaken all, and followed thee; what shall we have therefore?" (Matt. 19:27), the Lord used the number twelve in His answer. "And Jesus said unto them, Verily I say unto you, That ye which have followed me, in the regeneration when the Son of man shall sit in the throne of his glory, ye also shall sit upon twelve thrones, judging the twelve tribes of Israel" (vs. 28). Here the number twelve, the number of Jesus' disciples, is used symbolically of the perfect reign and rule of Jesus yet to come.

Jesus spent a night in prayer before He chose the twelve. "And it came to pass in those days, that he went out into a mountain to pray, and continued all night in prayer to God. And when it was day, he called unto him his disciples: and of them he chose twelve, whom also he named apostles" (Luke 6:12, 13).

Much could be said about the character and personality of the twelve. They were all men who, first of all, had to be saved. They were lost men who were won to Christ, with the exception of Judas Iscariot, who feigned Christianity until the dark hour of his infamous betrayal. They were men from various walks of life. Some were from public life, as Matthew Levi, the tax-collector, while others were obscure fishermen.

They were human. They sunk to the lowest when they all forsook Him and fled in the midst of His most crucial hour, but they rose to the highest when they were willing to die for Him and did! We will try to let the sermons on each of them address the subject of the character and personality of the twelve.

During the twelve-week period in which these sermons were preached, hundreds were saved and baptized.

Table of Contents

Chapter I

Jesus and the Twelve

"And he ordained twelve, that they should be with him, and that he might send them forth to preach." —Mark 3:14.

The calling of the twelve did not take place at the very initial stages of his public ministry, which we could suppose started with His baptism by John in the Jordan. Some try to show that the appointment of the twelve took place before the preaching of the Sermon on the Mount. This position is assumed from the expression in Matthew 5:1, "...his disciples came unto him," but then Matthew was not called until the record of Matthew 9:9. Other students of the Scriptures believe He called the twelve at about the halfway point of His three years of public ministry.

However, the formulation of the twelve started very near the beginning of His public ministry. A concise study of the Gospels would show that He began to save members of the twelve almost immediately after His baptism. It appears that some disciples were introduced to Christ the very next day after His baptism. "Again the next day after John stood, and two of his [John's] disciples; And looking upon Jesus as he walked, he saith, Behold the Lamb of God!" (John 1:35, 36).

The expression, "the next day," means the day after His baptism or perhaps the day before His baptism as the context of John 1:28-34 would clearly show. One of the two was Andrew who finds his own brother Simon and brings him to Christ. Philip and Nathanael were also saved at the same time. All of the disciples were first saved then called. Jesus had performed public miracles and preached the Sermon on the Mount before Matthew was called. "And as Jesus passed forth from thence, he saw a man, named Matthew, sitting at the receipt of custom: and he saith unto him, Follow me. And he arose, and followed him" (Matt. 9:9).

Before Jesus called the twelve He spent a night in prayer. It was a most significant event in the public ministry of Jesus. Before He chose the twelve, many followed Him and were called disciples.

"And it came to pass in those days, that he went out into a mountain to pray, and continued all night in prayer to God. And when it was day, he called unto him his disciples: and OF THEM he chose twelve, whom also he named apostles." —Luke 6:12, 13.

The twelve were special. They were also called apostles and were especially ordained into His cabinet or apostolate as our text clearly indicates. They were the twelve most significant men ever assembled together. They were all, Judas Iscariot excepted, destined to die as martyrs for the cause of Christ. John was to be inspired to write five of the twenty-seven New Testament books. James the less wrote one book and Peter wrote two. We cannot be certain but Judas (not Iscariot) might have been the author of the epistle of Jude. Matthew wrote the book of Matthew. Perhaps nine of the twenty-seven inspired books known as the New Testament were written by members of the twelve. They were very close to Christ. He claimed a relationship to His disciples more spiritually intimate than His relationship to His own human family.

"Then one said unto him, Behold, thy mother and thy brethren stand without, desiring to speak with thee. But he answered and said unto him that told him, Who is my mother? And he stretched forth his hand TOWARD HIS DISCIPLES, and said, Behold my

mother and my brethren! For whosoever shall do the will of my Father which is in heaven, the same is my brother, and sister, and mother.'' —Matt. 12:47-50.

I. THE TWELVE INSTALLED

"And he ordained twelve, that they should be with him, and that he might send them forth to preach.'' —Mark 3:14.

Six Greek words in the New Testament are translated ''ordain'' in various instances. There are some fifteen words in the Greek New Testament which are translated ''appoint,'' a close synonym of ''ordain.'' The word used in Mark 3:14, however, is *epoinase,* which means to make or appoint.

In common language it is saying that Jesus made these twelve men disciples or appointed them as such. Some say that this ordaining did not take place until after the resurrection of Christ in John 20:22, when Jesus ''breathed on them, and saith unto them, Receive ye the Holy Ghost.'' This position, however, is untenable. It is true that the disciples were filled with the Holy Spirit at Pentecost and enjoyed greater power with God than ever before. They were, however, appointed as disciples during His public ministry and ordained as such. Jesus made reference to this ordination near the very close of His public ministry in His Paschal discourse.

''Ye have not chosen me, but I have chosen you, and ordained you, that ye should go and bring forth fruit, and that your fruit should remain'' (John 15:16).

This passage applies to all of God's own, but verse 15 would imply that a special reference is being made to the twelve disciples. He is talking directly to a group of men to whom He had made known all things which He had heard from the Father. Since He is to go back to the Father soon, He ordains and appoints them to go out to the world and win souls and bear fruit that would last for all of eternity.

II. THE TWELVE WERE INVITED—THOUGH UNFIT

It is important to see that Christ did not call people because of some special gift or ability they already had. He called them according to His own sovereign wisdom and purpose. "And when it was day, he called unto him his disciples: and of them he chose twelve, whom also he named apostles" (Luke 6:13).

It is a prominent truth of the Scriptures that He does not call people because they are fit but He fits people because they are called. The call of God is the most important factor. The Lord calls everyone to be saved and to serve but there is a special call of God which comes to certain people. He does not call everyone to preach but there is a definite and special call of God to be a preacher of the Gospel. The fact that the Scripture says, "...whom also he named apostles," shows that this was no general call but a specific call.

Everyone was not called to be an apostle. It is generally accepted that an apostle was one who had to have been an eyewitness to the person of Christ.

"Even as they delivered them unto us, which from the beginning were eyewitnesses, and ministers of the word."—Luke 1:2.

"For we have not followed cunningly devised fables, when we made known unto you the power and coming of our Lord Jesus Christ, but were eyewitnesses of his majesty."—II Pet. 1:16.

There are no apostles today as these men and others were, for none of us have seen Christ in the flesh as they saw Him. Paul was an apostle and had seen Christ. "And last of all he was seen of me also, as of one born out of due time" (I Cor. 15:8).

The point I am trying to make is that the disciples had a special and distinct and divine call from Christ Himself. Jesus did not call angels to do His work but He called men! This is another affirming instance in the holy Scriptures that God calls and uses human agency in His mission of evangelizing the world.

III. THE TWELVE WERE INSTRUCTED

There appeared to be a constant program of instruction and teaching between Jesus, the greatest Teacher who ever walked on earth, and the inquiring minds of the disciples.

In a sense, the Sermon on the Mount was, for the most part, spoken to the disciples, though it is for all of His own. "And seeing the multitudes, he went up into a mountain: and when he was set, his disciples came unto him: And he opened his mouth, and taught them, saying..." (Matt. 5.1, 2).

This program of instruction was an on-going process. "And it came to pass, when Jesus had made an end of commanding his twelve disciples, he departed thence to teach and to preach in their cities" (Matt. 11:1).

The expression, "had made an end of commanding his disciples," refers us to the instruction given to them as recorded in Matthew 10:1-42. He instructed them to go out and preach to the "lost sheep of the house of Israel." He sent them out to win souls and to minister to the sick and demon-possessed.

He taught them in that chapter that God supplies the needs of those whose lives are wholly given to making known the Word and work of God. He told them that "the workman is worthy of his meat."

He instructed them to preach that He was near and men could come to know Him as the one sent from God to be their Saviour.

He taught them to appreciate the good homes into which they would enter, and at the same time be aware of the fickleness of human nature.

He warned them of persecution, but at the same time assured them that the Spirit of God would teach them what to say. He told them that God would speak through them. "For it is not ye that speak, but the Spirit of your Father which speaketh in you" (Matt. 10:20). How surpassingly wonderful!

He warned them of the hatred of the world, but comforted them with the assurance of the power and love of the heavenly Father.

He challenged them with the responsibility of cross-bearing, but consoled them with the promise of heavenly reward.

What a wonderful Teacher is Jesus! No wonder that on one occasion His would-be captors said, "Never man spake like this man" (John 7:46).

Even in Nazareth where He was hated, some "wondered at the gracious words which proceeded out of his mouth" (Luke 4:22).

The twelve were not men of letters but men of learning. They were products of the Bible Institute of Jesus and when later their hearts were set on fire, their heads were saturated with heavenly truth. They were men with a zeal according to knowledge.

Measured by all the standards of pedagogy, Jesus was the greatest Teacher this world has ever had. And measured by all the standards of learning, these twelve had been taught in the school of highest learning. The truth they acquired was not earthly and transient but heavenly and eternal. In the school of Jesus, both teaching and learning took place.

IV. THE TWELVE WERE EMPOWERED

"And when he had called unto him his twelve disciples, he gave them power against unclean spirits, to cast them out, and to heal all manner of sickness and all manner of disease." —Matt. 10:1.

The most inhuman and impossible task ever given to a group of men was that which Jesus gave to the twelve; to preach to the lost sheep of the house of Israel, to control unclean spirits, and to heal all manner of sickness and disease. Jesus did not ask them to do these works with human energy. He gave them power.

The wonderful thing about doing the work of the Lord is that He not only tells us what He wants done, but He furnishes us with the power with which to do it. Carrying out the Great Commission of taking the Gospel into all the world to every creature, is totally impossible without divine power.

The disciples used this power. They enjoyed great success in the work the Lord asked them to do. "And the seventy returned again with joy, saying, Lord, even the devils are subject unto us through thy name" (Luke 10:17).

However, they lost the power the Lord had given them. The man with the lunatic son whom Jesus eventually healed brought him first to the disciples but the disciples did not have power to cast the demons out of the stricken son. The father said to Jesus, "And I brought him to thy disciples, and they could not cure him" (Matt. 17:16). When the disciples asked the question, "Why could not we cast him out?" (vs. 19), Jesus answered them plainly; "Because of your unbelief. . . Howbeit this kind goeth not out but by prayer and fasting" (vss. 20, 21).

So it appears that the disciples lost their power because of weak faith and their failure to pray and fast. God's workmen should remember that we may have the power of God but it can be lost. How tragic the loss of power once used and enjoyed!

It is interesting to note that the Lord gave His disciples power soon after they were chosen, and He gave them power again after He rose from the dead and after He ascended back into the presence of the Father.

"But ye shall receive power, after that the Holy Ghost is come upon you: and ye shall be witnesses unto me both in Jerusalem, and in all Judaea, and in Samaria, and unto the uttermost part of the earth." —Acts 1:8.

"And they were all filled with the Holy Ghost. . . . "— Acts 2:4.

Peter preached with this power on the day of Pentecost to Jews only and to Gentiles in the house of Cornelius. He had the power to raise the dead and heal the lame man at the Gate Beautiful. The twelve had power to witness daily, win souls, and continue their ministry even under such great persecution as Christians have ever endured.

Oh, the Lord's servants need to tarry until endued with power from on High. It is impossible to win souls, build churches, evangelize the world and be completely true to the Lord and His Word without the power of God. How wonderful to preach with His power and see God work in a miraculous way!

V. THE TWELVE WERE IMPERFECT

Apart from the call and work of Christ in their lives, the twelve were neither gifted nor good. They were men of faults and of like passions as all human beings. Peter denied Him with such vehemence that did we not know what the Bible says, we would think him unsaved. James and John, with pride, asked for the chief seats in His coming kingdom, causing indignation amongst the rest. One sold Him to His enemies for thirty pieces of silver. And all forsook Him in the hour of His greatest agony (Mark 14:50).

Thomas refused faith without sight. Philip and Andrew would not believe that little is much when God is in it, until they saw the Lord multiply the small lunch of a lad and feed the hungry thousands. They trembled in the face of the stormy sea and hesitated at times to obey His commands immediately.

No, they were not perfect. The only perfect one, clothed with a fleshly body, that this world has ever known was Jesus. There is no perfect Christian, church, or preacher. All are enfeebled by the flesh, so much so that the greatest Christian cried out, "O wretched man that I am! who shall deliver me from the body of this death?" (Rom. 7:24).

How marvelously these imperfect men grew into His likeness! They became spiritual giants. They laid the foundation for the church and died for the Founder and Head of that glorious organism. The twelve are an example of His sustaining grace and keeping power. They became living models of spiritual growth. They who trembled at the raging sea, defied kingdoms, kings and armies for the cause of Christ in the earth. Boldness became their bulwark and love, the badge by which they were known "Now when they saw the boldness of Peter and John, and perceived that they were unlearned and ignorant men, they marvelled; and they took knowledge of them, that they had been with Jesus" (Acts 4:13).

"That they had been with Jesus" was one of His holy purposes in calling them in the first place. "And he ordained twelve, that they should be with him" (Mark 3:14). These twelve imperfect men, Judas Iscariot excepted, fulfilled God's holy purpose for calling them out and setting them apart for the intimate cabinet of the Lord Jesus Christ.

VI. BEFORE THEIR CALL, THE TWELVE WERE INCONSPICUOUS

It appears that only the traitor, Judas Iscariot, was from Judaea. The other eleven disciples were apparently from Galilee, referred to as the Northern Province. History infers that the people of Galilee were generally less sophisticated, less educated and usually less mannerly and more rude than Judaeans. Their speech was individualistic and easily recognizable.

Perhaps Peter, James and John had substantial livelihoods and perhaps Matthew profited from his extortionism as a tax-collector. But generally speaking, they were poor and unlettered. This, no doubt, was a part of the glorious design of the Lord so that all the glory for their eventual success and notoriety should be the

Lord's. Usually God works in this manner. "For ye see your calling, brethren, how that not many wise men after the flesh, not many mighty, not many noble, are called" (I Cor. 1:26).

God's Word does not say "not any," but "not many" such are called. The verses that follow teach us why the sovereign God follows this plan in the calling of men for His own work. "But God hath chosen...that no flesh should glory in his presence" (1:27, 29).

God delights to save and use the unlikely ones. The Mary Magdalenes, the bigoted rabbi such as Saul of Tarsus, the woman at the well, and the maniac of Gadara are examples of this divine principle. He delights to demonstrate how He can use the weak and base instruments when surrendered to His will.

I would never have chosen Gideon to be a general and David to be a giant killer, but God's ways are as high above the ways of men as the heavens are above the earth. Let us rejoice that the Father calls the weak and unworthy and trains them in His own school. "Let the brother of low degree rejoice in that he is exalted" (James 1:9).

VII. THE TWELVE WERE ENDEARED

"Now before the feast of the passover, when Jesus knew that his hour was come that he should depart out of this world unto the Father, having loved his own which were in the world, he loved them unto the end" (John 13:1). Blessed is the expression, "having loved his own which were in the world, he loved them unto the end." We are told that "unto the end" actually means "to the uttermost." He loved them with a love which surpasses human ability to describe. He loved them so deeply that He washed their feet as if they were children. That little flock of men were precious to Him. Shortly after He told the parable of the fool who died the night he counted his riches, acting as if he would live forever,

He said to His disciples, "Fear not, little flock; for it is your Father's good pleasure to give you the kingdom" (Luke 12:32).

Jesus taught His disciples what He wanted them to know and sometimes it included rebuke. When He predicted the denial of Peter, what sweet words of love and comfort He left with Peter: "Simon, Simon, behold Satan hath desired to have you, that he may sift you as wheat: But I have prayed for thee, that thy faith fail not: and when thou art converted, strengthen thy brethren" (Luke 22:31, 32).

"I have prayed for thee." With tender love and excelling grace, Jesus prayed for one whom He already knew would deny Him. He prays for us also. He is our Advocate at the throne of grace. In His high priestly prayer rendered up to the Father before He died, He promised to pray for me! "Neither pray I for these [the twelve] alone, but for them also which shall believe on me through their word" (John 17:20).

One of the most touching incidents in the Gospels is that which is recorded in John 18:19. "The high priest then asked Jesus of his disciples, and his doctrine."

Jesus started to answer him about His doctrine but never mentioned His disciples. He declined to air their imperfections to the ungodly world. Even though Jesus sometimes rebuked them privately, He never embarrassed them openly. With tender love He carried them as a shepherd carries his sheep in his bosom. They were endeared to Him with a love far surpassing the limitations of the very strongest human love on earth.

Behold, how Jesus loved the twelve! Behold, what manner of love He has for His body, the church! "Husbands, love your wives, even as Christ also loved the church, and gave himself for it" (Eph. 5:25).

The twelve were installed, invited, instructed, empowered, imperfect, inconspicuous and endeared. They were the most unique, extraordinary and individualistic twelve men ever identified as a corporate body that the world has ever known.

"And he ordained twelve, that they should be with him, and that he might send them forth to preach."—Mark 3:14.

Chapter II

Simon Peter, a Rock for Christ

"And he brought him to Jesus. And when Jesus beheld him, he said, Thou art Simon the Son of Jona: thou shalt be called Cephas, which is by interpretation, A stone." —John 1:42.

A tremendous man walks out of the pages of the Word of God and appears upon the stage of human history. He is mentioned by name as many times in the New Testament as the Apostle Paul is mentioned. The Holy Spirit has imprinted indelibly upon the pages of the New Testament this man's name. Strangely enough, he and Paul are mentioned almost an equal number of times in the New Testament. Approximately 150 verses or passages narrate the account of the salvation, call, ministry, personal life, failures and victories of this great man. Some authors have given him the appellation, Peter, the man unusual.

The Lord dealt with him in a special and unusual way. He had unusual experiences. He walked upon the water, preached on the day of Pentecost, and raised a person from the bonds of death. He was more controversial than any of the other disciples. He rebuked Jesus and Jesus rebuked him.

"Then Peter took him, and began to rebuke him, saying, Be it far from thee, Lord: this shall not be unto thee. But he turned and said unto Peter, Get thee behind me, Satan: thou art an offence unto me: for thou savourest not the things that be of God,

but those that be of men.''—Matt. 16:22, 23.

He had a controversy with the Apostle Paul. ''But when Peter was come to Antioch, I withstood him to the face, because he was to be blamed'' (Gal. 2:11). He cut off a man's ear defending the Lord in Gethsemane, then watched the Lord place it back in miraculous healing power.

Peter was genuinely converted, unusually controversial, amazingly colorful, completely human, and deeply consecrated.

Peter is a historical figure religiously. You will not read more about any Bible character than has been written about the Apostle Peter. Millions erroneously believe that he was the first Pope, the Bishop of Rome. Millions have been led to believe that he died at Rome and his bones are buried in Saint Peter's Cathedral where a great altar has been erected. Also a great bronze statue of Peter is found there where millions have kissed his feet until they have almost been kissed away.

He was a great Christian with tremendous courage who sometimes displayed cowardice. He seemed always to have an answer or a word to say. Sometimes his words were sublime, as when he identified the Lord as the Son of God:

''He saith unto them, But whom say ye that I am? And Simon Peter answered and said, Thou art the Christ, the Son of the living God. And Jesus answered and said unto him, Blessed art thou, Simon Barjona; for flesh and blood hath not revealed it unto thee, but my Father which is in heaven.''—Matt. 16:15-17.

His words were ridiculous at times, as when he wanted to stay on the Mount of Transfiguration forgetting the needy souls in the valley below: ''Then answered Peter, and said unto Jesus, Lord, it is good for us to be here: if thou wilt, let us make here three tabernacles; one for thee, and one for Moses, and one for Elias'' (Matt. 17:14).

Yes, Peter always had an answer; and he urges us to have one also. "But sanctify the Lord God in your hearts. and be ready always to give an answer to every man that asketh you a reason of the hope that is in you with meekness and fear" (I Pet. 3:15).

It is unwise to judge Peter's life simply on the basis of his failures. When we look at his whole life, we come to believe that he was one of the greatest Christians who ever lived. He was good at repenting. This is the difference between good Christians and mediocre Christians. Some people fail and sin against God grievously and never seem to repent. But Peter repented with a broken heart and bitter tears. "And Peter remembered the word of Jesus, which said unto him, Before the cock crow, thou shalt deny me thrice. And he went out and wept bitterly" (Matt. 26:75).

It has been conjectured that Peter was about twenty years older than Jesus. He might have been about forty-five when Jesus died. He was one of the favored three who were taken into a closer intimacy with Jesus. The New Testament tells us much about this bombastic, rigid, courageous, yet humble Christian man.

I. HE HAD MET AND ACCEPTED THE LORD JESUS CHRIST

Peter was won to Christ by his brother Andrew. When Andrew heard John the Baptist say, "Behold the Lamb of God!" (John 1:36), he went immediately to Peter to tell him that he had found the true Saviour, the Lord Jesus Christ. How blessed are the words Jesus spoke to Peter when Andrew "brought him to Jesus": "Thou art Simon, the son of Jonah; [John] thou shalt be called Cephas, which is by interpretation, A stone" (John 1:42).

Peter's natural name "Simon" means instability or vacillation. Jesus knew then that Peter would fail Him in the crucial hours of His trial and crucifixion, but He said, "Thou shalt be called Cephas" (stone). Jesus promised to change his life from instability to stability, from vacillation to rigidity. It was a prophetical state-ment, about the kind of a Christian God was going to make this fisherman from the shores of Galilee. He was saved instantaneous-ly, but it took three years for the Lord to make him like a stone.

There is such a thing as instantaneous salvation, but there is no such thing as instant spirituality. Yes, it is true, he unwisely used a sword, warmed at the Devil's fire, followed afar off, and cursed and swore that he was not of Jesus' company. But some three years or more after he was saved, he stood like an immovable rock and preached about Jesus on the day of Pentecost. He grew in grace and he made mention of it in his epistles: "But grow in grace, and in the knowledge of our Lord and Saviour Jesus Christ. To him be glory both now and for ever. Amen" (II Pet. 3:18).

Peter did not become a rock upon which Jesus built His church. Theological battles have been fought for centuries over this issue. We are not just Protestants, we are Bible Christians and our heritage does not begin with a man such as Luther and his Reformation. Our spiritual heritage dates back to Jesus Christ who said, "...upon this rock I will build my church" (Matt. 16:18).

This chapter describes a pivotal point in the earthly ministry of Jesus. It is here He teaches that He must go to Jerusalem, suf-fer many things, die on the cross, then be raised from the dead. It is here that He asks the question, "Whom do men say that I the Son of man am?" (vs. 13).

Men were willing to believe in a miraculous restoration to life of John the Baptist, but they were not willing to believe in the miraculous incarnation and deity of Jesus Christ. God had made Peter to believe and know that Jesus was the Son of God. The words of Jesus which followed Peter's sublime testimony constitute one of the most controversial matters in the history of Christiani-ty: *"And I say also unto thee, That thou art Peter, and upon this rock I will build my church; and the gates of hell shall not prevail against it."*

Did Jesus promise to build His church upon Simon Peter? He most certainly did not! He said, "Thou art Peter" [petros, a small stone] ". . . upon this Petra [a huge mass of stone] I will build my church."

Jesus never promised to build His church upon Peter but upon Himself as the "living stone," "the chief corner stone," "the rock that was smitten." It was to be builded upon "that spiritual Rock. . . and that Rock was Christ" (I Cor. 10:4). Peter was prominent in the early days of the church but he was not preeminent. The foundation of the church is not on Peter but on Christ. *"For other foundation can no man lay than that is laid, which is Jesus Christ"* (I Cor. 3:11).

The controversy does not end with verse 18, but continues through verse 19. Poor, deluded religious people have been taught for centuries that Jesus gave Peter the keys to Heaven. "And I will give thee the keys of the kingdom of heaven: and whatsoever thou shalt bind on earth shall be bound in heaven: and whatsoever thou shalt loose on earth shall be loosed in heaven."

Jesus said to Peter, ". . . and I will give unto thee the keys of the kingdom of heaven." The kingdom of Heaven is not necessarily heavenly; it is earthly. It is of Heaven, but it is not the church. Matthew 13 clearly teaches that there are both tares and wheat in the kingdom of Heaven—both saved and lost. The difference between the saved and lost is that the saved (wheat) have heard the Gospel and believed it unto salvation and have been born again. The lost (tares) only have an empty profession. They are religious but lost.

Keys are used to open doors, and the keys given to Peter were to be used to open the door of faith to both Jews and Gentiles. Peter used the key when he preached the Gospel to the Jews on the day of Pentecost and to the Gentiles in the house of Cornelius.

Peter did not have the keys any more than did John or Paul.

He used them first and thus was favored by the Lord because of his great confession. He had no authority over other believers. The Gospel of Christ is the determinant factor which binds or sets free on earth, and that determination is recognized in Heaven.

If a lost person should request water baptism, it is a binding thing that we do not baptize people unless they can give a testimony that they have been saved. This binding on earth is certainly condoned and recognized in Heaven. If one who has been saved requests baptism, it is binding that we baptize them. Heaven also recognized this transaction.

II. PETER GREATLY ATTACKED BY SATAN

"And the Lord said, Simon, Simon, behold; Satan hath desired to have you, that he may sift you as wheat: But I have prayed for thee, that thy faith fail not: and when thou art converted, strengthen thy brethren." —Luke 22:31, 32.

Jesus plainly announced to Peter that Satan was launching an attack against him. In reference to Satan, Jesus used the personal pronoun, "he"—"he hath desired to have you." The Devil is not merely an evil influence or wicked force, he is a person. Satan's attack against Peter was also an attack against Jesus.

You read one time in Matthew 16 where Jesus and Simon Peter are again engaged in conversation. Simon Peter in that chapter says of Jesus, "Thou art the Christ, the Son of the living God." In that same chapter Jesus said to them, "I must go to Jerusalem, suffer many things, be killed, and be raised again the third day." When Peter heard Jesus say this, we read, "Then Peter took him, and began to rebuke him, saying, Be it far from thee, Lord: this shall not be unto thee" (vs. 22).

Here Peter says to Jesus, "Jesus, You just said that You are going to the cross." He said, "Be this far from Thee, Jesus, You do not need to go to the cross." Peter wanted Jesus to set up His "kingdom right then and rule on earth. He did not want Him to go to the cross. Jesus said to Peter then, "Get thee behind me, Satan . . . for thou savourest not the things that be of God, but those that be of men" (vs. 23). Right then Jesus said, "Peter, the Devil is speaking through you." Satan sought to lay hold upon the life of this great Christian and to fight him bitterly.

Peter needed to learn three things. When he said to Jesus, "You do not need to go to the cross," he needed to learn that there is **no redemption without blood.**

Last Sunday, the parents of one of our young ladies came down front following the service and said, "We are so glad that our daughter is in a church where the blood of Jesus Christ is honored and preached." I said truthfully and sincerely, "We don't know anything else in this church but the story of the blood of Jesus Christ."

Peter learned that. In his first epistle he said, "Forasmuch as ye know that ye were not redeemed with corruptible things, as silver and gold, from your vain conversation received by tradition from your fathers; But with the precious blood of Christ, as of a lamb without blemish and without spot" (I Pet. 1:18). The Devil did not want Peter learning that there is no redemption without blood.

Second, Peter needed to learn that there is **no glory without suffering.** When he wrote his first epistle, he had learned this and he said, ". . . the sufferings of Christ, and the glory that should follow" (I Pet. 1:11). He said to Jesus, "Have Your glory now; no cross, no suffering before the glory and exaltation."

Third, Peter needed to learn that there is **no fruitfulness without death** and giving of one's self. John 12:24, "Verily, verily, I say unto you, Except a corn of wheat fall into the ground and die, it abideth alone: but if it die, it bringeth forth much fruit." So Satan sought to get hold of the life of Simon Peter, as he wants control of the life of every Christian in this room tonight! This personal Devil went after Peter in his thinking and in his actions. He sought to thwart the plan of God for Simon Peter as he will do to every Christian if he can. "Submit yourselves therefore to God. Resist the devil, and he will flee from you" (James 4:7).

Simon Peter was a man who sometimes wanted to do things in the power and energy of the flesh. That is what the Devil wants all to do. He does not want us to trust God and work in the power of the Spirit. I read in John 18:10, "Then Simon Peter having a sword drew it, and smote the high priest's servant, and cut off his right ear. The servant's name was Malchus." That night in the garden when Jesus was to be taken, and the night before His crucifixion, when they came to arrest Him, Simon Peter drew a sword and said, "They shall not take Jesus! They shall not lay hands upon Him!" and struck a servant of the high priest and cut off his ear. Jesus had to rebuke him, "Put up again thy sword." He said, "Thinkest thou that I cannot now pray to my Father, and he shall presently give me more than twelve legions of angels?" (Matt. 26:53). Jesus said to Peter, "...they that take the sword shall perish with the sword." The Devil was still trying to get the life of Simon Peter. Finally Peter gained a great victory.

Jesus said to all of the disciples, "The shepherd will be smitten, and the sheep will be scattered abroad" (Matt. 26:31). He was saying, "You are going to deny Me." Most of them did not say anything, except Peter who said, "Though all men shall be offended because of thee, yet will I never be offended." Jesus said, "Verily I say unto thee, That this night, before the cock crow, thou shalt deny me thrice."

Sure enough: that night, the last night Jesus spent on earth, three times Peter said, "I don't know Jesus. I'm not a Christian. I'm not one of His." That night he denied Him three times.

No wonder that in I Peter 5:8 the Apostle Peter warned, "Be

sober, be vigilant; because your adversary the devil, as a roaring lion, walketh about, seeking whom he may devour.''

Let me say it again tonight: Satan wants the life of every Christian in this room! Even though your soul has escaped him, your life has not escaped him yet! Satan wants your life. He wants control over it. The pitiful thing is that Satan does get control many times. Peter was greatly attacked of the Devil.

III. PETER WAS GREATLY USED OF THE LORD

I am thrilled and encouraged when I see how the Lord used Simon Peter. Jesus said, "But I have prayed for thee, that thy faith fail not: and when thou art converted, strengthen thy brethren'' (Luke 22:32). The word "converted" means "turned back again.'' He was already saved. Simon Peter did just that. In John 21, Jesus said to Peter, "Feed my sheep." Peter later said, "Feed the flock of God which is among you...." (I Pet. 5:2).

The Lord used Simon Peter, after the crucifixion of Jesus first to introduce the Gospel to the Jews on the day of Pentecost. Thousands were saved. Then He used him to introduce the Gospel officially to the Gentiles in the house of Cornelius when hundreds heard and believed and were saved. He wrote two epistles. He comes down to us tonight as a man who believed something and stood for something. Peter was greatly used of God.

IV. PETER BELIEVED IN MIRACLES

Do you believe in miracles? Many say, "I don't believe anything I can't explain in a natural and rational way." Simon Peter was not that kind of a Christian. He believed in miracles.

In Matthew 14:29 the Lord told the disciples to go over to the other side. They were going from Bethsaida, where a great miracle had been wrought, across the Sea of Galilee, a distance of about seven or eight miles. As they started across the sea, a great storm arose. In the midst of the storm and the wind they saw a figure walking on the water. Some said that it was Jesus. Some said that it did not look like Him—in the stormy sea they could not tell. Simon Peter said, "Lord, if it be thou, bid me come unto thee on the water" (vs. 28). Jesus said, "All right, Simon Peter, come unto Me on the water." Knowing Simon Peter, that impetuous, bombastic-type of personality, I think he backed up and took a running start, then jumped out of the boat into the Sea of Galilee and started walking to Jesus.

I remember once seeing a picture on a beautiful stained-glass window in North Carolina. It did not show Peter walking on water but sinking under the water, with his hand lifted, about to drown. The Lord was reaching out to take his hand. It happened that way. Before it happened, Peter walked on water! He believed in miracles! So do I. I believe in a miracle-working God!

A Christian said to me yesterday, "I just feel like quitting the whole thing." I said, "No Christian should ever quit! Not as long as there is a miracle-working God in his life!" God will and does work miracles. Simon Peter believed that the Lord could work miracles.

He made a mistake. But no one should spend thousands of dollars to magnify a mistake. I would like to see a stained-glass window showing Peter walking on water. No one else other than Jesus, ever walked on water. Peter did because he believed in the miraculous things of God.

That helps to explain something. In Acts 12 Herod had his men behead James, another disciple. Then Herod proceeded to take Peter, intending after Easter to behead him. Peter had no reason to doubt him, since the soldiers had just taken off James' head.

Knowing that Peter believed in miracles, a soldier was put on each side, and he was chained on each side to a soldier. A guard was out at the locked gate, watching to see that he stayed in jail until Easter, when his head would roll.

The Bible tells us that Peter lay down that night and went sound asleep—so sound asleep that God had to send an angel to the jail to wake him! "Wake up, Simon." Simon opened his eyes and looked right full in the face of an angel, who said, "Get up, Simon Peter." The chains fell off and the gates opened and he walked out free! Why? He believed in miracles. O God, give us a faith in Jesus that there is a miracle-working God! Peter believed in miracles.

V. HE WAS SPIRIT-FILLED

I will close with this, though I am not nearly through with Simon Peter. I wanted so much to talk to you tonight about Peter and his connection with Rome, but I will have to put that off for a time.

Simon Peter was a Spirit-filled Christian. In Acts 1:8, Jesus said, "But ye shall receive power, after that the Holy Ghost is come upon you...." He told the disciples to tarry in the Upper Room until they were endued with power from on High. Peter did that and he became a great, Spirit-filled Christian. That is why Acts 4:13 says, "Now when they saw the boldness of Peter and John, and perceived that they were unlearned and ignorant men, they marvelled; and they took knowledge of them, that they had been with Jesus." These Sanhedrin said, "There is something supernatural, miraculous, about that man."

He said to a cripple sitting at the gate who was over forty years old, "Rise, stand up on your feet." When he who had been crippled all of his life leaped up, they said, "There is something about that man. In whose name did you work that miracle?" Peter said unto them, "By the name of Jesus Christ of Nazareth, whom you crucified, whom God raised from the dead.... There is none other name under heaven given among men, whereby ye must be saved" (Acts 4:10, 12). What was supernatural about him? He had the power of the Spirit of God in his life.

Mrs. Malone was showing me the other day a personal hand-written letter that we had received years ago from old Dr. Charles Weigle, the great songwriter who lived to be over ninety. This great man, this great Christian wrote, "No One Ever Cared for Me Like Jesus," and many other beautiful songs. One song he sang right here said, "Jesus is a garden of roses to me." The reason for writing that song was because of something that actually happened in California years ago.

A group of business people were meeting in a banquet hall. A man present that night loved flowers, roses especially. He had spent the whole day at a great rose farm walking among the roses and smelling them, looking at them, enjoying them.

Here at this great banquet room someone said, "I smell roses."

"But there are no roses in this room."

"There may not be, but I tell you, I smell roses in this room!" After hearing of this, then they heard of this man who had the fragrance of roses all over him because he had spent the whole day in the rose garden. Dr. Charles Weigle wrote that beautiful song, "A Garden of Roses Is Jesus My Lord to Me."

The truth is, they who walk with Jesus, live with Him and are filled with His Spirit, give off a fragrance, a power like Spirit-filled Peter. What an example! May we be the same kind of Christian as he.

"And he brought him to Jesus. And when Jesus beheld him, he said, Thou art Simon, the Son of Jonah; thou shalt be called Cephas, which is by interpretation, A stone."—John 1:42.

VI. HE WAS CONTROVERSIAL

Simon Peter was the most controversial of all the disciples. Without a doubt we can truthfully say that Peter was probably the most controversial figure in the New Testament. He was more controversial than the Apostle Paul. I have not heard people argue about the Apostle Paul nearly as much as I have about the Apostle Peter. He was controversial even in the Bible. He was controversial even in history.

The Roman Catholic church and the Protestant churches (though we were a church before the Protestant Reformation) have much controversy over the Apostle Peter. We came from the Bible times as a church, not just from Martin Luther. The Catholic church and Protestant churches have argued about Simon Peter for hundreds and hundreds of years. There is no figure in all the Bible nor in all history who has been as controversial as Simon Peter in the minds of both Catholics and Protestants.

If it were not for the fact that there are great Bible truths involved that have to do with salvation by grace, the keeping power of the Lord and other great doctrines, all of us would say, "So what? We don't want to argue about Simon Peter." But there are great truths involved.

I was thinking today about something that I had not thought of before. It was about Simon Peter and we will just say the Roman Catholic church. By the way, in our church we see many Catholics saved. We love them and want to see them saved, just like we want to see lost Methodists, lost Baptists and lost sinners of any kind saved. I was thinking today that if a Catholic was absolutely straight on the subject of Simon Peter, he could no longer be loyal to the Roman Catholic church. It is a controversial subject about a controversial figure.

Catholics believe that he was the first Pope, that he was never married, and that he was infallible. They believe in apostolic succession, celibacy, and so forth. All of these controversial things are centered around the life of a man, not Jesus but Simon Peter. If a Christian could understand just exactly the truth from the Bible about Simon Peter, then he would have it straight. Both Roman Catholics and Protestants have some prejudices about Peter.

Catholics say, as I have mentioned, that he was a Pope and that he was never married. They believe a priest should never marry. I have told you about the statue that I have seen. My family and I have seen the statue of Peter in the Vatican in Rome. It is a large statue made of solid bronze. There it is. Catholics for years and years have kissed one of his feet until there are hardly any toes left. Half of the foot is worn away. I have seen them come, touch it and kiss it with their lips. This has been done so many millions of times until that solid piece of metal has literally been kissed away from the great piece of statuary of the Apostle Peter. Catholics believe him to be a perfect one, the first Pope. Around him are teachings of the priesthood, celibacy and all that goes with it. They are prejudiced in that way. They think Simon Peter is buried in the Vatican, claiming to have found his bones. Of course there is absolutely no Bible basis for these beliefs.

Protestants are also prejudiced. Most Protestants say, "Simon Peter never saw the city of Rome." I want to show why it could not be possible that Simon Peter was the first Pope. Also, why he was not even supreme as an apostle and was never in the place of leadership that is given him in the minds of many Catholics.

Simon Peter is the one in Acts 10 who went to the Gentiles with the Gospel. He was arraigned before the church in Jerusalem: so it did not think him infallible, perfect. When he got through at Caesarea, in the house of Cornelius, the church said, "Simon Peter, you come back here to Jerusalem and appear before this church to be examined on this action that you've taken! You've gone to uncircumcised Gentiles and preached the Gospel to them! We hear that many of them have been saved! You come before the church and give an account of this!" That group did not think he was perfect; they did not look upon him as a Pope. They did not think he was a leader of the church. Rather, "You come and be arraigned before this church."

The Scripture that I read to you tonight is of Simon Peter standing before the church at Jerusalem literally defending himself so he will not be cast out of the believers at Jerusalem. So he was arraigned before the church at Jerusalem.

Another strange thing in the Bible is that the Apostle Paul once quite severely reproved the Apostle Peter. He just talked straight about it. When he wrote his letter to the Church at Galatia, he brought this up because it has to do with salvation by grace. Let me read it to you. In Galatians 2 it is talking about the Lord revealing the Gospel to Paul. Look at verse 11: "But when Peter was come to Antioch, I withstood him to the face, because he was to blamed. For before that certain came from James, he did eat with the Gentiles: but when they were come, he withdrew and separated himself, fearing them which were of the circumcision."

Paul did not think Peter was perfect. Paul did not look upon Peter as a leader of the whole church. Paul did not think that Simon Peter was a Pope and Paul said, "I had to face him in a matter and help him to see the truth about his relationship to the Gentiles. I had to face him with what he believed and what I believe about the Jew first, then the Gentile being saved. Both are saved the same way, both are saved by the same Christ. I had to make him see that this was according to the teaching of the Bible." So Paul did not think Peter was infallible in any sense of the word.

James is shown in chapter 15 of the book of Acts as the leader of the church, not Peter. Acts 13 and 14 have to do with the missionary journeys of Paul, Barnabas and others. They went out and they got a lot of Gentiles saved. It was just like Peter did in the house of Cornelius. When they got back from these successful and tremendous missionary journeys, the church in Jerusalem called them to appear just like it had called Peter after he preached the Gospel to the Gentiles in the house of Cornelius, saying, "Paul, you and Barnabas had better go to Jerusalem and stand before them." They went up and gave an account, and came to an agreement. Now I read in Acts 15:13, "And after they had held their peace, James answered, saying, Men and brethren, hearken unto me." In most of the rest of the chapter James, the ruling elder in the church of Jerusalem, takes charge.

When people say that Simon Peter was a Pope and talk about apostolic succession and the popery being handed down by Peter, they are wrong. Acts 10:25 shows that Simon Peter would let no one worship him as they do the Pope today. If they tried to kiss his feet, as they kiss the statue's feet, he would refuse it. Acts 10:25, 26, "And as Peter was coming in Cornelius met him, and fell down at his feet, and worshipped him. But Peter took him up, saying, Stand up; I myself also am a man." He was saying, "Don't worship me, I'm a man just like you!" He never claimed to be a Pope.

There is a lot of discussion on whether Peter was ever in Rome and will be, I guess, until the Lord comes. I want us to see a few things tonight on whether he was ever in Rome. I will lead up to something I hope will be of interest to you.

He was not in Rome when Paul wrote the book of Romans. In Romans 16, Paul wrote to the church at Rome from Corinth and mentions approximately 35 friends. They were those already in Rome and some who were at Corinth from where he wrote. He never mentions the name of the Apostle Peter. When Paul wrote the book of Romans, Peter was not in Rome. If you will read the Roman Epistle, you will conclude that in spite of the fact that these were believers in Rome and small churches in homes, no one became the head of the church in the city of Rome.

In Romans 15:20 Paul was talking about coming to Rome and preaching the Gospel: ". . . lest I should build upon another man's foundation." In other words, "I will not build on another man's foundation." So there was no large foundation there, just a little scattered group of believers. There was no large church and no leader. Peter was not there when Paul wrote the epistle to the Romans. He was not in Rome when Paul was prisoner at Rome. In that Roman prison, Paul wrote Philippians, Philemon, Colossians and Ephesians and never once did he mention Peter.

If you went to Rome tonight and to the Mamertine Prison, a plaque in the wall would give you a traditional record. You would see some steel bars embedded in the wall. The Apostle Paul was probably chained to these bars. From that prison he wrote some of these epistles. It also would say that Peter and Paul were prisoners together in that prison. In Paul's four letters—Philippians, Philemon, Colossians and Ephesians—he never mentioned Peter as his companion. While Paul was there and probably to the time of his martyrdom, the Apostle Peter was not in Rome. Perhaps Peter might have gone to Rome at some time in his later years.

Don't think all of this is unimportant. First of all, Peter wrote two epistles. First Peter 5:13 says, "The church that is at Babylon, elected together with you, saluteth you; and so doth Marcus my son." It may sound like it has nothing to do with Rome. Believers back in the year 130 A. D. believed that when Peter wrote of the church of Babylon, he was talking about the church at Rome. They believed that he was there when he wrote the epistle of I Peter. But there is no record in the Bible of there being a New Testament church of any kind in Babylon.

There is a lot in the Bible about false religion and ecclesiasticism being called "Babylon." From Genesis 11 to the book of Revelation, all kinds of false religions and ecclesiasticism and false worship is called in the Bible "Babylon." Revelation 17 and 18 say that the world ecumenical church that is being formed is "Babylon" and called an abomination unto God. Dr. A. T. Robertson, one of our greatest Greek and Bible scholars, said, 'There is no question that when Peter wrote I Peter 5:13, he was writing about the church at Rome and no doubt wrote from Rome.'

From that period unto this there have been some great Bible-believers who have written some wonderful things. All interpreted this the same way. All believe that Peter was in Rome after Paul was. A man named Eusebius interpreted it the same way, that is, that Peter wrote from Rome about the church of Rome. Clement of Alexandria, Ignatius, Eusebius, Dionysius of Carthage, Tertullian, Jerome, and many others before 200 A. D., wrote about Peter being in Rome. You say that is traditional. Well, a lot of things are traditional and are not to be believed unless you can prove them from the Bible. But some things that are traditional are true.

An example of this is that I did not see Columbus when he discovered America, but that he did is a historical fact. It has been handed down for all of these years by church fathers and Christian writers that Simon Peter was at Rome and became a martyr there. There are some things that can be true even though they are not in the Bible. The Bible does not say that two and two are four, but you and I know that is true. I will give you an example about how something can be traditional, yet be the truth.

There is in the home of my mother down in north Alabama a bed well over a hundred years old. It was handmade by my great-grandfather Vinson down in Cherokee, Alabama, perhaps 140 years ago. It is still in good condition and is still used in the home of my mother. I have slept in it many times. I did not see my great-grandfather Vinson make that bed; but Grandmother Hargett, who was a Vinson, told my mother that her father, when she was a wee child and before she knew anything about it, made that bed. My grandmother was born well over one hundred years ago. She has now gone to be with the Lord. My grandmother told my mother that her father made that bed. My mother told me that her grandfather, my great-grandfather, made that bed. It has wooden pegs.

It is sound, sturdy, well-made. My great-grandfather was somewhat of a carpenter. He did beautiful work with cedar and with other kinds of woods.

There is not any question that my great-grandfather made that bed. It is not written in any book, it is not written in the Bible, but there is no question about it. It is handed down traditionally. It has passed through three or four mouths to come to you tonight. There is no question but that it is true.

Accurate, historic tradition says that Simon Peter was at Rome which probably would have been 60 or 70 years after his death. He was probably crucified somewhere in his sixties. It was told that when Nero was persecuting Christians, Peter was persuaded by believers in Rome to leave the city. They said, "You're going to be martyred. Leave the city!" So he started out.

Out at the edge of the city, as tradition has it, he began to pray and talk to the Lord. As he talked to Him, the Lord appeared and told him to go to the Gentiles. Peter said, "Jesus, are You here at Rome? Where are You going? What are You doing?" It seemed that Jesus said to Peter, "Peter, I came here to Rome to be crucified again." Peter knew what He meant—that in him, in Simon Peter who was to be a martyr, there was to be another demonstration of one dying on the cross.

Peter turned and went back into the city. When they took him to crucify him, accurate tradition says that he said, "I'm not worthy to die like Jesus died, on a cross with His head toward Heaven. 'In all things that he might have the preeminence.' I can't die like that, turn me upside-down." Tradition says they nailed his feet to the top of the cross and his hands down toward the world. Blood ran and Peter died, just like Jesus died.

It is pretty accurate tradition that he became a martyr for Jesus Christ in the city of Rome. Where he was buried, nobody knows. Whether his bones have been discovered, nobody knows. They would not be worth any more than my bones or your bones if they found them tonight.

Jesus told Peter that he would die the death of a martyr in John 21:18, 19:

"Verily, verily, I say unto thee, When thou wast young, thou girdest thyself, and walkedst whither thou wouldest: but when thou shalt be old, thou shalt stretch forth thy hands, and another shall gird thee, and carry thee whither thou wouldest not. This spake he, signifying by what death he should glorify God."

VII. PETER, A GREAT BELIEVER IN THE SECOND COMING OF JESUS CHRIST

Simon Peter looked for the return of the Lord. He wrote that "there shall come in the last days scoffers, walking after their own lusts, And saying, Where is the promise of his coming?" He said, "People will laugh at the second coming, but the Lord is coming back again." He went on to say, "But the day of the Lord will come as a thief in the night..." (II Pet. 3:3, 4, 10). Then he closed his last written words with: "Looking for and hasting unto the coming of the day of God, wherein the heavens being on fire shall be dissolved, and the elements shall melt with a fervent heat?" (vs. 12).

Peter looked for the second coming of Jesus Christ when all things will be made right for the child of God. That is what I am looking for tonight. Are you? "Even so, come, Lord Jesus."

"And he brought him to Jesus. And when Jesus beheld him, he said, Thou art Simon, the Son of Jonah; thou shalt be called Cephas, which is by interpretation, A stone."—John 1:42.

Chapter III

Andrew—a Man's Man

READ: Matthew 4:12-25.

"And Jesus, walking by the sea of Galilee, saw two brethren, Simon called Peter, and Andrew his brother, casting a net into the sea: for they were fishers."—Vs. 18.

This is not a record of the conversion of Andrew. We want him to step out of the pages of the Word of God so that we can become more familiar with him. This is a definite call from the Lord to be a soul winner, to follow Jesus, to be a disciple. That call came after he was saved.

I don't think Scripture really tells us when Andrew was saved. The first chapter of the book of John tells us about John the Baptist and his ministry. Andrew had been listening to John and no doubt had believed the message that John preached. No doubt he had followed on in water baptism. One day John saw Jesus come and the Bible tells us that God had said to John, "I will tell you how you can recognize Jesus. One day One will come to you to be baptized. He will be different from all the rest. When you see One come into the River Jordan to be baptized and the Spirit like a heavenly dove descends and remains on Him, then John, you will know that is Jesus Christ, My Son and the Saviour of the world."

One day Jesus came to be baptized of John and the Holy Spirit in the form of a heavenly dove came upon Him. Not only that, but the heavens opened and God, with an audible voice, said, "This is my beloved Son, in whom I am well pleased; hear ye him" (Matt. 17:5).

Andrew heard all of this. He heard John when John said, "Behold the Lamb of God, which taketh away the sin of the world" (John 1:29). Under the ministry of John the Baptist, Andrew believed on the One who was soon to come and soon to die for his sins, and Andrew was saved.

I call Andrew "a man's man," for "Andrew" means "manly." Strong, healthy, physical Andrew was a man's man as well as God's man. He is mentioned in only twelve verses in the New Testament, but what an important character and what a great man he was!

He wrote no books. You will not read of any letters that Andrew wrote, like Paul and Peter wrote, or James and John wrote. We read of no sermons Andrew preached. We read a few statements he made, but he wrote no books that we know of, no letters, preached no sermons that the Spirit of God recorded. We read of no miracles that he wrought. But what a tremendous man of God he was!

He did such a great work that I believe no person in all the New Testament, perhaps with the exception of the Apostle Paul, will have a greater reward than Andrew. He did such a tremendous work. He was noted for bringing people and introducing them to Jesus. There are three chapters in John that mention him. In chapter 1 he brings Simon Peter to Jesus. Chapter 6 tells where the great miracle of the feeding of the five thousand is wrought. There he brings a lad to Jesus. In chapter 12 he introduces the seeking Grecians who said, "Sir, we would see Jesus." Andrew brings them and introduces them to Jesus.

I believe that Andrew gives us a true picture of Christianity.

Many people say, "I am saved. I am a Christian. I know the Lord. I have accepted Christ into my life," but they do not give a true picture of Christianity as Andrew did.

The true picture of Christianity, as it is set forth in the Bible, is not only a saved person, but a serving person. The Bible teaches that a Christian is not only saved, but his life is invested in serving the Lord Jesus Christ. Andrew was not only saved but always serving—a true picture of Christianity.

Just suppose you wanted to learn the Bible. Suppose you started in Genesis and studied about every character in the Bible, starting with Adam and going right down through the Bible to John on the Isle of Patmos. You would know the Bible because God has clothed His truth, like garments of clothing, upon individuals. When you study them, you see what the Bible has to teach us.

For instance, regeneration: Jesus said in John 3:3, "Except a man be born again, he cannot see the kingdom of God." To whom did He say that? To a religious man by the name of Nicodemus. "Nicodemus, you have religion. You pray, you worship, but you have never been saved, never been born again." When you think of regeneration, you think of one who was religious but lost.

Justification is that God has declared a believer righteous in His sight. Justification means a truly saved person stands in the eyes of God as clean as if he had never sinned. When I think of that, I think of an Old Testament man by the name of Abraham. The Bible says in Romans 4:3, "Abraham believed God, and it was counted unto him for righteousness." God justified Abraham who believed in God and believed His Word.

When I think of grace, this great doctrine of the Bible, unmerited favor, I think of Noah. In Genesis 6:1-7 God looked down upon a generation and said, "I am going to destroy them. The end of all flesh is come before Me. I am going to destroy the world with a flood." Genesis grace. Grace is undeserved favor, unmerited favor, undeserved kindness. Noah found grace in the eyes of the Lord.

Let me ask you something. You have been saved by grace. Why did God save you? No human reason, no good reason, nothing good in you made God want to save you. He saved you even when you were a sinner and did not deserve to be saved. That is grace.

When I think of grace, I think of a man whom God has clothed His truth of grace around his life.

When I think of atonement—the guilty saved by the blood of the innocent—I think of Isaac. He was born in a miraculous way, not like Jesus, but a miracle like the birth of Jesus was a miracle. Isaac was born to a man who was one hundred years old and to a woman ninety years old.

One day Isaac takes a bundle of wood and with his father climbs Mt. Moriah. He is about to be sacrificed, but God stays the hand of Abraham that held the knife and says, "Look, Abraham, there is a ram in the thicket. Take that lamb, put it on this altar and substitute it for Isaac."

When I think of atonement, I think of Isaac.

When I think of the law, I think of Moses. John 1:17 says, "For the law was given by Moses, but grace and truth came by Jesus Christ."

When I think of the flesh, I think of the first king of Israel, Saul, a man who exemplified the evil and the power and strength of the flesh.

When I think of religion, I think of a young rabbi who hated Christians, a young rabbi who said, "Touching the law of God, I am blameless." When I think of religion, I think of Saul of Tarsus who one day got saved and became the Apostle Paul.

When I think of prophecy, I think of John to whom the Lord said, "I will reveal to My servant things which must come to pass."

When I think of the twelve disciples, I realize that every good virtue, every manner of service, every strength, every weakness, every sin, every form of dedication to God is all wrapped up in the twelve disciples of our Lord Jesus Christ. God clothes His truth about human beings.

Now, let us see Andrew. If you could see him today, if you could learn something about this great Christian, it would change your life. It could be a life-changing experience for you to become biblically acquainted with this disciple named Andrew.

I. ANDREW WAS A SAVED MAN

Andrew was a saved man, the most important thing that could ever be said about anybody. I don't care how successful a person is in politics, in commerce, in war, or in any phase of life; if you cannot say he is a saved person, he has missed the greatest thing in life.

Andrew was saved by the death of the Lord Jesus Christ. You say, "But when Andrew was saved, Jesus had not yet died." True. In chapter 1 of John, John the Baptist is preaching. One time he said, "Behold the Lamb of God, which taketh away the sin of the world." Then verse 36 says, "Behold the Lamb of God!"

Andrew heard him preaching that the Lamb of God is coming and has come. Jesus, God's Son, is going to die, the latchet of whose shoes he was not worthy to unloosen. Andrew said, "I believe his message, that one is coming to die for me who will be my Saviour." Andrew believed on Him and His work on the cross, and was saved. Andrew was saved by looking forward to the cross. You and I are saved by looking backward to the cross and trusting Jesus Christ.

Andrew was saved by the testimony of another. I wish God would grip our hearts with this. Like every one of us, Andrew was saved by the testimony of another. Beyond any doubt, I was saved by the testimony of a Methodist preacher, Brother Campbell, down in north Alabama more than 38 years ago. Andrew was saved by the testimony of John the Baptist, who said, ''The Lord is here. The Lord is coming. He is going to die for every one of us. Jesus Christ, God's Son, has been given.'' Andrew believed his testimony.

Some people will never be saved unless they are saved by your testimony. Do not sit there and say, ''I am no preacher. The souls of people do not depend on me.'' There are those in this world today whom only you can win. A lot of people, who do not know a preacher, have never met a preacher; but they know you. Their only hope of hearing the Word of God and being saved may be by your testimony.

Andrew was saved by hearing the Word of God. Did you know that it is impossible to be saved apart from the Word of God? John the Baptist preached the Word of God and Andrew was saved as a result of the Word of God.

I have had folks say, ''What about the heathen who have never heard?'' You cannot be saved without the Word of God. I know the Bible says God reveals Himself as the Creator, His handiwork is seen throughout the heavens, and heathens can see that. But to believe on the Lord Jesus Christ and to be saved, one must hear the Word of God. Romans 10:17 proves that: ''So then faith cometh by hearing, and hearing by the word of God.''

That is why we have no message but the Bible. We have no philosophy but the Bible. We have no teaching but the Bible. We have no message, no sermon, but the Word of God because people cannot be saved without hearing the Word. John preached that Word and the Bible plainly teaches you cannot be saved without hearing the Word of God.

Andrew was saved as he made a public confession, or I will say that he made a public confession because he was truly saved. No doubt Andrew was baptized of John in the River Jordan.

Andrew was not what some people call a "secret Christian." I don't think there is such a thing. Jesus said, "Whosoever believeth on him shall not be ashamed" (Rom. 10:11).

Andrew was baptized publicly. He made a public confession of his faith.

A lot of people have said, "Preacher, I will be a Christian, but I'm not going to walk down that aisle." When you realize that you are lost and when you really want to be saved, you will not hesitate. I have seen people run down the aisle. I have seen people almost jump over somebody to get out in the aisle and make a public confession of Jesus Christ. Romans 10:9, 10 says,

"That if thou shalt confess with thy mouth the Lord Jesus, and shalt believe in thine heart that God hath raised him from the dead, thou shalt be saved. For with the heart man believeth unto righteousness; and with the mouth confession is made unto salvation."

God says that you believe in your heart and confess with your mouth. I would remind you that Jesus said,

"Whosoever therefore shall confess me before men, him will I confess also before my Father which is in heaven. But whosoever shall deny me before men, him will I also deny before my Father which is in heaven."—Matt. 10:32, 33.

A man or woman says, "Yes, I am saved, but I'm not going to say anything about it. Yes, I am saved, but I'm not going to follow the Lord in baptism. Yes, I am saved, but I'm not going to make a public confession of it." Jesus says, "He that denies me before men, him will I deny before my Father which is in heaven."

Andrew was a saved man. I do not know exactly when it took place, but I want to tell you the greatest hour in Andrew's life was the day when he realized that by faith in Jesus Christ he was called a child of God.

There have been some great hours in the history of the world but the greatest is when you come to know Jesus Christ as your personal Saviour.

I am thinking of a great hour in my life. I was saved, as I have already indicated, by an old-fashioned, circuit-riding Methodist preacher. I can hardly wait to get to Heaven to talk to him. When I have talked to Jesus a few thousand years and sat at His feet, I'm going to look up that old circuit-riding Methodist preacher. He had a chicken coop on the back of his old Ford car. About the only pay he ever received was when somebody would take a chicken, tie its legs together with a piece of cloth and bring it to him to throw in the chicken coop on the back of his car. People would bring him a bag of beans or a sack of potatoes.

This old, country Methodist preacher—oh, how he loved God! I have often thought of where I would be today if it were not for him; if he had not said, "Tom, I love you. I want you to be saved. I am interested in you." The greatest hour of my life was when I came to know the Lord Jesus Christ.

Fortunately, I met somebody else shortly after that, a young man by the name of Paul Lupo, then a senior in Bob Jones College. Paul Lupo was a preacher. It looked as if God sent him no one else but me. He set in on me.

"Tom, you ought to go to a Christian college." Here I was, a boy in overalls and tennis shoes and this man saying, "You ought to go to college."

"I have no money."

"You have God, don't you? You have just been saved, haven't you?"

"But I am timid. I don't even want to face people."

"But you have God. You are saved and your life is important."

For one solid week, he never let up on me. The few souls I have won—I should not say few, for, thank God, there have been thousands—I must say that in Heaven Paul Lupo will get a share of those. The greatest hour in my life was when I became introduced to Jesus Christ.

Andrew was a saved man. Are you saved today? Do you know the Lord Jesus Christ as your personal Saviour? Have you made public confession of Him? Have you heard His Word and believed?

Andrew was a saved man.

II. ANDREW WAS A DEVOTED MAN

Something else I like about Andrew is, he was devoted to the Lord. I do not know of anything more needed today in fundamental, Bible-believing churches than what I am about to say to you.

First of all, Andrew was a friend of John the Baptist. Listen, you couldn't be a friend of John the Baptist without paying a price. John the Baptist was not the most popular preacher in the world. He would put his finger under people's noses and tell them what they had to do. He would not baptize some people who would come to be baptized. "You have not repented yet. When you repent, then you can get baptized." He talked about moral things until finally he got his head cut off.

But Andrew said, "Oh, John the Baptist is a man sent from God. God is with him. I am going to be his friend." Andrew was his friend and a devoted Christian.

He started immediately to follow Jesus. Will you let me just read it right out of the Bible? "Then Jesus turned, and saw them following, and saith unto them, What seek ye? They said unto him, Rabbi, (which is to say, being interpreted, Master,) where dwellest thou?" (John 1:38).

Jesus turned and here was Andrew. He was saved now. Seeing Jesus moving along, he just starts following in His steps, he and another disciple. Jesus turned around and said, "What are you looking for?"

Andrew said, "Jesus, we would like to know where You live."

No one had to ask where Pilate lived. No one had to ask where Herod lived. No one had to ask where Caiaphas lived. But, they had to ask Jesus where He lived. Jesus said, "The foxes have holes, and the birds of the air have nests; but the Son of man hath not where to lay his head" (Matt. 8:20).

When Andrew wanted to know where Jesus lived, Jesus said, "Come and see" (John 1:39). Jesus said for Andrew to follow Him and Andrew did. Jesus slept out under the stars at night; no pillow for His head but a stone; no canopy to cover Him but the heavens above. Andrew said, "I am going to follow Jesus."

When the first nightfall started to come, maybe Andrew said, "Where are we going to sleep tonight?" Jesus said, "Follow me." Out yonder on the lonely mountainside, Jesus lay down and pillowed His head upon a stone, prayed a prayer to His heavenly Father, then said, "Sit down over there, Andrew."

Andrew was a devoted man. How devoted are you to Jesus today? Do you love Him? Do you desire to be with Him? Come rain or shine, are you devoted to the Son of God? Andrew wanted to live with Jesus. He was not interested in just knowing His address; he wanted to live where Jesus lived.

I have read verses in the Bible which give me this information. For instance, Mark 1:29, "And forthwith, when they were come out of the synagogue, they entered into the house of Simon and Andrew, with James and John." There is Jesus. One day Andrew and Peter said to Jesus, "Jesus, come on over to our house. We want You to live in our house." Is Jesus in your home?

Study people in the Bible. Some folks let Him in their heart and others let Him in their heart and home. Does Jesus live in your home? What about the Bible in your home? What about prayer in your home? What about Christian living in your home? If you are not a good Christian where you live, you are not a good Christian sitting in church.

God looks upon me and my wife. If we are not Christians at 1045 Dover Road, we are not fit to be called Christians anywhere else. Home-spirituality is needed in America today and all that goes with it. Andrew was devoted to Jesus.

I read where Jesus said to this man, "Follow me, and I will make you fishers of men" (Matt. 4:19). Andrew said, "Here I come, Jesus." Are you devoted to Jesus Christ?

I went to school with a young man in 1935. He is a fine preacher today. This young man came from a family who were not Gentiles. When he got saved down in North Carolina, he was working in a men's clothing store as a clerk. He went to hear a preacher preach. He preached the Word of God, told about Jesus and this young man was saved. The Spirit of God spoke to his heart. He recognized the Lord Jesus Christ as his personal Saviour and trusted Him and was gloriously and wonderfully saved. When folks would come in that store, they could see a difference in him. He would tell them, "Now, I have been saved. I know the Lord now as my personal Saviour."

One day the store owner, who also was Jewish, came and said to him, "Now listen, I do not believe in Jesus Christ, so don't mention His name in this store. If you believe in Jesus Christ and you are going to be telling people you are a Christian, then you will have to find another place to work." He said, "All right, I will." He lost his job because he was a Christian.

About that time his parents said, "Now listen! You are embarrassing us. We are not Christians. We don't even believe that Jesus is the Son of God. A good man, yes; a good teacher, yes; but not the Son of God. You are embarrassing us by telling people you are a Christian."

He said, "I love you, my mother and my father. I love you more than anything on earth. But Jesus has saved me. Jesus has given me happiness and peace in my life. So I am going to follow Jesus no matter what it costs me."

They said, "Well, you cannot live here and continue to embarrass us before all of our relatives, our friends and our business associates."

He said, "I will follow Him no matter where He leads."

God led him to Bob Jones College and I met him shortly after this. He is a preacher of the Gospel today. He was so devoted to Jesus that he said, "If I cannot work where I can let people know I am saved, then I will not work there." He was so devoted to Jesus that following Jesus meant the loss of his family. He was saved, he was devoted to Jesus Christ.

How devoted are you? Would you give up a job for Jesus if that is what it took? Would you give up earthly ties? Would you sever them if it were said to you, "If you are going to be a Christian, you cannot be a member of this family"?

Are you devoted to Jesus today? Andrew was saved and devoted. That is what God wants from every one of us.

III. ANDREW WAS A SOUL WINNER

I believe Andrew was a soul-winning man. Andrew was listening to John the Baptist. The ministry of John the Baptist, by the way, was influential in Andrew's coming to know the Lord. Andrew was saved by the witness and testimony of another. Just about everybody is saved by the witness of another. I think we can say there is no one saved without the witness of another. God speaks through people, their life, their testimony. Andrew was saved through the witness of John the Baptist. When John the Baptist saw Jesus walking across the plains of Jordan, he said, "Behold the Lamb of God that taketh away the sin of the world." What did Andrew do? The first thing he did after his conversion was to get somebody saved.

I have had folks ask me, "Preacher, when people first get saved, ought they go out preaching and talking to other people?"

Certainly! Jesus not only permitted it, but recommended and condoned it.

No one had any greater results than the woman who met Jesus at the well. Are you listening? That woman was gloriously saved at the noon hour. Then she goes back into the city. People knew her, knew she had had five husbands.

When you are saved and changed and have God in your life, people will know it. You won't have to prove it. When they see you are saved, they will listen to your testimony.

She went back to bare witness. Then shortly Jesus sees her coming with a multitude of Samaritans from the city of Samaria, coming because of her testimony. A new convert got people saved. That is the way God worked in Bible times and that is the way it ought to be today.

The first thing Andrew said was, "I want to tell somebody about my new-found joy, this new life I have. It is so thrilling and wonderful, I want others to know it." He used his testimony in winning Simon Peter and others to Jesus Christ.

Let me say this for your encouragement. You don't have to be a theologian to win people to the Lord. There are several wonderful ways to talk to people. For instance, thousands have been saved by what we call the "Romans' Road." Just get in the book of Romans and start in chapter 3 with the outstanding verses about how all have sinned, how you need to be saved, and the gift of God; but you do not have to know the "Romans' Road" to lead somebody to Christ.

Proof of that is the maniac of Gadara. He was a raving man. Chains could not bind him. Jails could not hold him. Society could not change him. He was out among the tombs at night and all the citizens feared him.

One day they saw him like they had never seen him before. They saw him sitting at the feet of Jesus. He had been without clothing, cutting himself, out among the tombs a raving maniac. But they saw him sitting, clothed and in his right mind. Oh, they marveled! This man had been saved, changed completely. That is what the Lord does. "Therefore if any man be in Christ, he is a new creature: old things are passed away; behold, all things are become new" (II Cor. 5:17).

A good dose of salvation is God's cure for a person in the matter of sin. He became a new creation in Christ. He said, "Now, Lord, I would like to follow You. Jesus, You have changed my life. What the Law and the efforts of human society could not do, You have done."

Anything that helps a man stop being a drunkard is good. I am not condemning the AA's and all such things, but there is but one cure for sin and that is Jesus Christ and His precious saving blood. That is what happened to that fellow. Now he says, "Jesus, I want to go where You go. I want to follow You."

Jesus said to that maniac of Gadara, in Mark 5:19, "Go home to thy friends, and tell them how great things the Lord hath done for thee...." Praise God, that is our message to give!

Do you want to win somebody to Christ? Tell them what great things the Lord has done for you. I know we use the Scripture, I know God wants us to learn and to grow in this matter of soul winning, but Andrew used his testimony. He just said, "Peter, we have found Him." "Nothing so profound about that," you say; but there is. He immediately began to use his testimony to win others to Jesus Christ. He literally learned soul winning from Jesus.

Listen carefully. I am not the greatest example in the world, not by any stretch of the imagination. I have seen hundreds and thousands of people saved, hand-picked and in public services, but I know my weaknesses and shortcomings. I could have won thousands more had I been "red-hot" for God. I want to tell you something, Jesus said to Andrew, "Follow me, and I will make you fishers of men."

There is only one way to be a soul winner and that is to follow Jesus Christ. If you are following Him, you will be a soul winner. If you arc not following Him, you will not be a soul winner. You cannot win souls and be out of step with the Son of God. The reason a lot of folks do not win people to Christ is because they are not following Jesus.

Andrew learned soul winning from Jesus Himself. Jesus said, "Follow me, and I will make you fishers of men." If you follow the Lord Jesus Christ, you are going to get around to thinking about getting others saved.

People criticize this church. Thank God for that! I would be the most disappointed preacher in the world if nobody ever criticized Emmanuel Baptist Church. I would wonder whether we had the Lord with us or not. People criticize the Emmanuel Baptist Church about all sorts of things. They say, "They are evangelistic." What is wrong with that? I thought Jesus was. I do not see anything wrong with being evangelistic. They say, "Well, they do not go deep in the Word." That is a lot of baloney!

It is like a fellow said to me one time, "How about the deep things?"

I said, "What deep things?"

"Well, Brother Malone, you know, the deep things."

"Yes, I know, but what are they?"

"You know—the deep things."

"Yes, but what are they?"

He didn't know either. He just wanted to act smart and play big and continue being a big hypocrite.

God is interested in people getting saved. A church where people are not saved is not a New Testament church.

When somebody says, "They are evangelistic out there," you

say, "Hallelujah!" "Praise the Lord!" "Selah!"

They say, "Just getting people saved is not enough." But it is the greatest thing, the first thing. You cannot teach them until you get them saved.

The first thing Andrew did was to become a soul winner. When a person gets saved, the next thing he ought to do is get baptized. Don't ever say to me, "Pray with me, Brother Malone, about getting baptized." I will not pray with anybody about getting baptized. God told you to do that and you ought to do it.

Then the Bible teaches that we are to fellowship with the people of God. Fellowship one with another in the reading of the Bible, in separation, in looking for His return—all of this is just being a good Christian. When you get this way, you are going to want to see people saved. If you are not in this way, then you are not going to want to. A lot of people sit back and watch somebody else do it, then criticize. If you are a Christian and you are not making an effort to lead somebody to Christ, God have mercy upon you!

Let me ask you: Have you ever won a soul to Christ? You cannot win your second one until you have won your first one.

I was trying to think the other day about the first soul I ever led to Christ. I think it was like this. When I went to Bob Jones College in September 1935, the first job I had was to be kind of like an athletic director for a junior high school. I would go in the afternoon for two hours. Then I had a night watchman's job. I was working day and night for big money. I mean, I was raking it in—25ᶜ an hour. I didn't know what to do with all of that money.

In an afternoon on the school grounds of a junior high school, a young girl came by. I said, "Are you a Christian?"

She said, "I am a Catholic."

I said, "Are you saved? Are you a Christian?"

"I do not know what you are talking about," she said. When

we had finished our responsibilities in athletics, between her house and the campus I led this Catholic girl to Christ. Probably she was the first soul I had ever led to the Lord.

A few days after that I got to thinking that a person ought to speak to somebody every day about Jesus. I got down on my knees in my room and started talking to the Lord. It was kind of like Ananias, big and pious, who said, "I will talk to anybody."

The Lord said, "Ananias, you go talk to Saul."

He said, "Lord, not him. He has been trying to kill everybody."

I prayed, "Lord, if You will help me, when I get up off my knees and leave this room, I am going to talk to the first person I come to."

Now listen, and it is true. I walked off the campus of Bob Jones College in Cleveland, Tennessee, and started toward downtown. There he stood—the biggest guy I had ever seen in my life, big, barrel-chested fellow standing there on the side of the road. Here stood this big guy. I began to try to convince myself that it would not be tactful and wise to speak to such a person as he. The Lord seemed to say to me, "Well now, you made the bargain. If you meant it, go ahead and speak to him. There is your first one."

I walked up to him. I didn't know that you had to say, "Nice day, isn't it?" I walked up and stood up under that big guy and, scared to death, looked up and said, "Are you a Christian?"

There was total silence. His big head dropped on his chest. I saw that his lips were trembling. "No, I'm not; but I ought to be. I live down here in Georgia. When I left this morning, my mother followed me out to the front gate of the yard and said, 'Son, you have never been saved and I want you to be saved. I am going to pray that today somebody will lead you to Christ.'" I never saw an easier person to lead to the Lord!

Have you ever led a soul to Christ? Why do you think God tells us so much about Andrew's soul winning? Is it because God wants you and me to be a soul winner?

Notice where he started—at home. A Christian ought to be able to witness to his own family. I have had people say to me (and I do not agree with this at all), "Now preacher, you go talk to my family. You know a fellow can't talk to his own family." You can if you are really saved. You can if you really care whether your family goes to Hell or not.

Andrew first went to his brother. I wonder how many of you have an unsaved mother? I know in this audience there are some whose mother—the one who brought you into the world—is lost and without God. Maybe a father is lost. I wonder how many of you have a son that has never been saved? Oh, darkest of hours will be that hour when you stand at the casket of an unsaved loved one. I wonder how many of you have a son or daughter or wife or husband not saved? God wants us to start at home.

When you study about Simon Peter, you will find he was so bombastic, so vivacious and such an outgoing personality even after he was saved. You get a glimpse, too, of what he was before he was saved. Simon Peter was some man. Andrew walked up to him and said, "Brother, I have found Jesus." He got no argument but was wonderfully saved. His testimony was immediately received by his brother. I like that. Yours will be too, when you, in sincerity, witness to a member of your family.

I read recently of a Chinese girl whose whole family was unsaved and steeped in false heathen religion. But she got saved. She was a bit fearful. She knew if she immediately said to her family that she was a Christian, she would be removed from the home and there was no telling what might happen to her. So she decided to wait awhile before telling them.

After a day or two her mother and father began saying to her, "You are different. Something has changed about you." All her life she was the spoiled child of the family. She always wanted her own way. If she did not get it, nothing was right. Now her parents said to her, "You are no longer spoiled. Your whole countenance has changed. You are so much sweeter. Something drastic has happened. What is it?" Then she told them, "I have been saved and Christ has come into my life." They believed her and her influence and testimony counted for Christ.

If a person is genuinely saved and is following Jesus, folks will listen when you talk.

That is the way it was with Andrew. When you get saved, baptized and are separated, looking for the Lord to come, living in fellowship with God's people, reading the Word, praying; with nothing between your soul and Jesus, when you talk, people will listen.

Andrew was a soul-winning man.

IV. ANDREW WAS INFLUENTIAL

I want to mention a fourth thing about Andrew and I do not know of anything more important to a Christian. Andrew was an influential man, a man of influence. He never wrote a book that anyone knows anything about. You do not read of his preaching any great sermons. He did not work miracles nor raise any dead that we know of, unless it was in conjunction with other disciples. But, we do know that Andrew was a man of influence.

I see him in chapter 6 of John. I love this kind of a fellow! In John 6, we read of the greatest miracle Jesus ever wrought—the feeding of the five thousand: "One of his disciples, Andrew, Simon Peter's brother, saith unto him, There is a lad here, which hath five barley loaves, and two small fishes: but what are they among so many?" (vss. 8, 9).

Think for a moment. Just before this, Jesus had said to Philip to try Philip, because Jesus already knew what He was going to do: "Whence shall we buy bread, that these may eat?" (vs. 5). Philip said to Jesus, "Two hundred pennyworth of bread is not sufficient for them, that every one of them may take a little'' (vs. 7).

About that time, Andrew began looking around, thinking, *If there is going to be a miracle wrought and these people are going to be fed, we have to start somewhere.* So he brought a lad to Jesus. It did not say a young man; it just said a lad, a boy. He had a little lunch in his hand and Andrew said, "Jesus, here is a lad who has five barley loaves and two dried sardines; but what are they among so many?''

Jesus took them and blessed them. Then the power of Heaven came upon what Andrew had brought to Jesus, and Jesus' greatest miracle was wrought, the only miracle recorded in all four of the Gospels.

For one thing, Andrew believed in influencing people to give to Jesus. You do not find many Christians like that. A lot of Christians, thank God, give to the Lord. That was not enough for Andrew. He went around saying, "Do you have something? Give it to Jesus. Whatever you have, you owe to the Lord. Give it to Jesus.''

He was a man of influence.

He believed in multiplying his life. Do you believe in multiplying yours? Do you believe your life ought to be multiplied in the lives of others? He believed in influencing people toward God and righteous living. Who could ever criticize what he did, for he said to a little lad, "Son, Jesus wants your loaves and fishes.'' He influenced a lad to give all to Christ.

Your influence is important. I am preaching to people who are saved people but some whose influence is like a withering blight. Wherever you find them, you find weakness all around them. Wherever you find them, you find criticism, disloyalty. Wherever you find them, you find people living sub-standard to what God and the church expect. You will face your influence at the judgment seat.

You go on and criticize the work of God and Christian people. Rebel against it. Go on and do it. Someday when you walk up in the white light of the holiness of the Son of God, you will be called to give an account of the deeds done in the body.

This influential man Andrew believed in starting with what he had, which was not much. That seems mighty insignificant—five biscuits, two sardines, and five thousand men besides women and children; probably fifteen or eighteen thousand people to be fed. A lot of people said, "You cannot do it with only that." But Andrew believed you could. So he brought them to Jesus while asking, "What are these among so many?"

I read a great commentator the other day who criticized him saying, "Oh, his disbelief." I cannot go along with that. When Andrew said, "Jesus, here is five loaves and two fishes; what are they among so many?" I think he was saying, "Jesus, when You get through with these, there is going to be a miracle wrought." There was. And twelve baskets left over!

I have often wondered about that—twelve baskets left over. Why? He fed all this multitude, started with five loaves and two fishes and gathered up twelve baskets full. I do not want to read into the Bible, but I will give you my opinion. I think the Lord said, "Gather up all these baskets full that nothing remain, nothing be wasted." Then I think He said, "Simon Peter, you take a basket. Andrew, you take a basket. John, you take a basket. Thomas, you take a basket. Nathanael, you take a basket. Philip, you take a basket. Both you James men each take a basket. Both you named Judas each take a basket. Matthew, you take a basket." Here are twelve disciples, everyone going home with a basket hanging over their shoulder full of loaves and fishes!

I can hear them now. Old Philip is saying, "Boy, if I live to be a hundred, I will never say it cannot be done again!" I can just hear old doubting Thomas (I have often asked my mother why she named me after that particular one who was always hanging a funeral wreath on every doorknob), "It cannot be done. We are all going to die. The ship is sinking. Man the lifeboats! There is no use! Everything is going down"—I can see him with his basket full saying, "Boy, I didn't think they could do it, but they did! Jesus did it." By these twelve baskets full left over, the Lord wanted to show that He could take a little and make much out of it.

I look back across more than thirty years when my wife and I walked out on this little dance floor of the Castle Inn building with no money, no promises, no support, no people—nothing! On our knees on that little dance floor we claimed it for God. Thank God, His Word has gone around the world as a result of it!

Little is big if God is in it! I think of Emmanuel Baptist Church and Midwestern Baptist College, where preachers are being trained to go out and build churches and are doing it and hundreds of people are being saved. I think of the many times when little groups of some of the dearest and sweetest saints in the world and myself would go over there in the weeds and sand and sometimes sleet and hail and snow, in the cold winter, get down on our knees and pray, "O God, raise up a training center here." God did!

I tell you, the same God who took five biscuits and two dried fishes can do it again! He has never changed. He is the same yesterday, today and forever.

Andrew was a man of influence.

I think of people who have influenced my life. I could mention the name of one or two great preachers. Dr. Bob Jones, Sr., influenced my life as no other has. I think of a man into whose life I walked thirty-four years ago, a humble Baptist deacon by the name of Earl Clemons who lived up at Flint, Michigan. As I look back on my association with Earl and his dear wife, I realize how much that man touched my life. For instance, in the early days of my ministry up at Leonard, Michigan, I met him in Flint where I held a revival meeting. I could tell you one of the greatest stories in the world about Earl Clemons.

I was in a church preaching and didn't have much sense. If I thought of something, I would preach about it. It is just like Sam Jones who said he had a "tom-cat" sermon. That was when he would "scratch everything." I didn't know any better. People were getting saved. The altar was full every night. Some of the people in that church got together with the preacher and deacons and said, "That guy is stirring up things and we ought to close this meeting. He has talked about this, he has mentioned that. We had better close this meeting and get that fellow out of here."

A Baptist deacon was sitting there who had a warm heart and a backbone like a railroad iron. He stood to his feet. He always carried a black Bible. He even carried it like he loved it! You never saw him without it. He stood to his feet and said, "No, we are not going to do that. But if you do, I will go out there next Sunday and tell everybody why you wanted this preacher run off and why you wanted this revival closed when scores are being saved. I will tell them you closed it because you could not take his getting on your sins."

They said, "Well, we don't want that to happen."

"Then, you had better forget about wanting to close this meeting."

I didn't know anything about this for a long time. If I had known something about it then, I probably would have run for my life.

That Baptist deacon had what it takes. He said, "This is what this church has needed, this is what God wants, and people are being saved. We are not letting this preacher go." He stood by me then and for years he has stood by me.

I remember times when I was seeking an answer from God. He would know nothing about it. He would come with that big black Bible and, with tears in his eyes, he would open that Bible and read somewhere while I sat there. He would read a verse or two, maybe a chapter. When he got through, I would say, "Praise the Lord! That is what I have been looking for! That is the answer!"

You say, "Well, how did he know that?" The Lord told him. He touched my life. He made me know that when you stand for God, God will stand for you.

How about your influence? Some folks influence other Christians the wrong way. They say, "You do not have to live up to standards. Do your own thing. Do as you please." If your influence is driving people away from God, you need to get right with the Lord.

Andrew was a man of influence.

V. ANDREW WAS A MISSIONARY

Andrew was a missionary. Andrew believed some wonderful things. In John 12, there was a great thing taking place. Lazarus had been raised from the dead and a great supper was being held in his honor. Folks came and people crowded around Jesus. In that chapter there were some Grecians who came and they said, "Sirs, we would see Jesus." Hearing them, Philip, for some strange reason, said, "Well, I had better find Andrew. Andrew knows how to take people to Jesus." So he found Andrew and told him, then both Andrew and Philip introduced these people to Jesus.

Andrew believed God loved everybody, not just the Jews. He believed God loved the whole world. That is what this Bible teaches, too. God loves men around the world no matter what their color. John 3:16, "For God so loved the world...." Peter, a Jew, said in the house of Cornelius, a Gentile, "God is no respecter of persons" (Acts 10:34).

He believed that God loved everybody. He also believed that he was responsible to get the Gospel to the whole world.

Not only that, but he recognized that many have hungry hearts. Here they were. He did not have to go and get them convicted of sin. They came and said, "Sir, we would like to see Jesus. We want to get where Jesus is. We want to meet Jesus."

A lot of people would like to know Jesus. Not all are hardhearted. There are broken hearts, tender hearts, hungry hearts.

I shall never forget one Sunday afternoon, one of the greatest afternoons of my life. My oldest daughter was about eleven. One Sunday afternoon we took a stack of cards and pencils and went calling, down one side of the street and up the other.

A young girl had caught fire while playing with some boys who were using gasoline to wash car parts. Somebody threw a match in it. She was one ball of fire. She came running by us. She would have been dead and in eternity, had we not stopped her and thrown her down on the ground. We put out the fire and took her home only slightly burned.

That afternoon we walked up on a porch and knocked on the door. A woman answered. Her head was bowed as she came. She opened the door and never said a word.

"My name is Tom Malone. I am from Emmanuel Baptist Church." That is as far as I got.

She said, "Oh, are you a preacher?"

"Yes."

She said, "Thank God! Will you come in? Oh, how we need a preacher! We need God in this home."

She took me by the arm and led me through the living room, through the dining room and into the kitchen. Standing at the sink was a boy in a soldier's uniform and with a knife in his hand. His head was bowed. He was trying to get the courage to take his life.

She boldly said, "That is my son. He wants to take his life."

I walked up to him and reached around and took hold of his

arm. He opened his hand and laid the knife in mine. I put it down. I got him by the arm and, with his mother weeping, led him back through the dining room into the living room.

The mother and her soldier boy were both saved that afternoon.

I did not have to say, "You are a wicked, lost sinner. If you take your life, you will go to Hell." His heart was hungry. So was his mother's.

I thank God I was in the right place at the right time!

Andrew believed God loved everybody and wanted them to be saved.

_____ Chapter IV _____

James, the Brother of John

READ: Acts 12:1-4.

"And he [Herod] _killed James the brother of John with the sword."_—Vs. 2.

I have seen these little tracts which give the record of what happened to the twelve disciples. Tradition says all of them, without exception, laid down their lives for the cause of Christ. They all became martyrs for the Lord Jesus.

We do not have to go to tradition to find out what happened to James, the brother of John. The Bible plainly tells us that James became a martyr for the Christ who saved him, the One whom he loved and followed for three and a half years.

Let me remind you that we are talking about one who enjoyed a special intimacy with our Lord. I have mentioned to you, in our character studies of these various disciples, that there were three whom, for some reason, the Lord took into His intimacy more than He did the others—Peter, James and John. James and John were brothers. The Lord said only to these three, "Come with Me into a special intimacy."

For instance, it is these three who went with Him when He raised the twelve-year-old girl from the dead. It is these three who went with Him on the Mount of Transfiguration. It is these three who went with Jesus deeper into the garden that awful night when

He was betrayed, when He prayed out there in the Garden of Gethsemane, "O my Father, if it be possible, let this cup pass from me" (Matt. 26:39). Recently, it occurred to me that the Lord was demonstrating three great truths to these three disciples.

For instance, when He took them into the garden and they heard Him pray, "If it be possible, let this cup pass from me," they saw His travail of soul: "And being in agony he prayed more earnestly: and his sweat was as it were great drops of blood falling down to the ground" (Luke 22:44). It looked in that crucial moment as if His soul would break from His body. That night the three saw the great truths of redemption, the Innocent about to die for the guilty, the perfect One about to die for sinful people.

When He took them to see the twelve-year-old girl raised, He was teaching them about the resurrection.

When He took them upon the mountaintop and was transfigured and Moses and Elijah appeared, He was teaching them about the second coming.

So you see, James is one who enjoyed these three special moments of intimacy with the Lord Jesus Christ. He enjoyed these three truths when Jesus gave an illustration of His redemption by the shedding of His blood, His justification by His being raised from the dead, and His glorious coming again when He shall come to claim His church unto Himself.

This man about whom we are studying now, James, the brother of John, is never mentioned apart from John. I do not know what the Holy Spirit is trying to tell us through this. Even here, when he is separated from John and is about to become a martyr for Christ, it says, "James, the brother of John."

James is saved and called. Matthew 4 gives the record of the day when Jesus walked along the shores of Galilee and saw Andrew and Peter casting their net into the sea, and He said to them, "Follow me, and I will make you fishers of men."

He went a little farther and saw James and John in a ship with Zebedee their father, mending their nets. He called them. Immediately they laid down their fishing nets and set out to follow Jesus.

James was always mentioned first. James was older than John.

Jesus was no touch-up artist. Here the Lord gives us a picture of this man. When you read about somebody out of the Bible, He paints the picture as it actually was.

If one of you ladies were to get your picture made, the photographer would say, "Come back and look at the proofs on such and such a day."

When you go back, you say, "Sir, see that big wrinkle right there? I want that removed. See that mole up there? Take that off. See that little wisp of hair that's out of place? Fix it up."

The photographer says, "Okay, you come back in two weeks and your pictures will be ready."

In two weeks you go back and you see a beautiful lady. It does not look like you at all. That is the way photographers do us about our pictures. He is a touch-up artist.

Not Jesus! He had them step out of the pages of divine inspiration, He pulled off all the veneer and said, "Here they are just like they were!"

I want you to see this man James just as he is.

I. JAMES WAS A ZEALOUS CHRISTIAN

I read in Mark 3:17, "And James the son of Zebedee, and John the brother of James; and he surnamed them Boanerges, which is, The sons of thunder." These men were enthusiastic. When Jesus saw them and knew them, He surnamed them. "Surname" means a name or epithet has been added to one's given name. For example, King Richard I of England was called Richard the Lionhearted. Jesus added to the names of James and John, "sons of thunder." Surname means an appendage to a name.

When Jesus saw Simon Peter, he had never before been called Cephas. Jesus surnamed him Cephas. And that is what He did to these two brothers, James and John. He surnamed them Boanerges, sons of thunder, because they were so zealous, so enthusiastic. He surnamed them because of their zeal for the things of God. We need that kind of Christians, those with some zeal and energy to exercise for the Lord.

You see this in two occasions when you think it might not have been the best thing.

You see it when John and James came to Jesus and said, "Master, we saw one casting out devils in thy name, and he followeth not us; and we forbad him, because he followeth not us" (Mark 9:38). In other words, "He was not in the twelve, he was not in our group, but he was casting out devils in Your name. We told him not to do it anymore."

Jesus said, "You did wrong," so to speak. He corrected the sectarian spirit in James and John. "For he that is not against us is on our part" (vs. 40).

Another time you see these two brothers as Jesus was going to Jerusalem with His face set. He knew that He was going there to die, to pay for the sins of the world. The villages and people saw His face set that way and they would not accept them. James and John came to Jesus and said, "Lord, wilt thou that we command fire to come down from heaven, and consume them, even as Elias did?" (Luke 9:54). To these two zealous, enthusiastic Christians, Jesus says, "I came not to destroy men's lives, but to save them."

Here were zealous Christians.

I say again, we need in the church of Jesus Christ a zeal on the part of God's people. We have so many lackadaisical Christians who are letting the world go to Hell. "Who cares anyway? Who cares if you build a great soul-winning church that will train people? Let it go to Hell; who cares?'' That is their attitude. Our churches today are filled with professing Christians who exercise themselves not one bit to get people saved and send the Gospel around the globe, as Jesus taught us it must be done!

Here are two zealous Christians. Christians need to be zealous about the souls of others. It is time God's people were zealous about the cause of Jesus Christ! It is time for the Lord's people to be zealous about the Bible. I believe the Bible. I believe it is God's Word! Any Christian should want the whole world to know that the Bible is God's Word! We should love it, believe it and seek to live by it. Zealous Christians were James and John.

I was saved in the Methodist-Episcopal Church of the south nearly 39 years ago. When I was first saved I heard tell about a young Methodist preacher and a Methodist bishop. The Methodist preachers almost revered the Methodist bishops.

One day a young Methodist preacher and an elderly Methodist bishop were walking down the sidewalk in a little community. That young Methodist preacher, wanting to make an impression on that bishop so badly, was trying to talk so piously and spiritually to him. All of a sudden a poisonous snake crawled out on the sidewalk. The old bishop was walking with a walking stick. The young preacher got so excited that he jerked that walking stick out from under the bishop's hand causing the bishop to fall. The young preacher took that walking stick and wore it out over that snake. He killed the snake but tore up the bishop's walking stick!

After it was over and the snake had been killed, realizing the old brother bishop's predicament, he got him by the hand and picked him up. The bishop, somewhat agitated by it all, said, ''You've ruined my walking stick. And you've caused me to fall.'' The young Methodist preacher picked him up and said, ''Sir, when I see snakes, I'll use anything I can get my hands on to kill them!''

Maybe he did not have all the knowledge he should have, but

he had zeal! Zeal is contagious. Paul said of the Corinthians, "...your zeal hath provoked very many" (II Cor. 9:2). Only God knows that we need today a zeal for Christ! These men had it. James was a zealous Christian.

"And he killed James the brother of John with the sword."

II. HE WANTED PRE-EMINENCE

I said to you that Jesus was no touch-up artist. Had some people written the biography of this man James, the man who gave his life for Christ, they would have mentioned not one thing bad about him. They would have found nothing selfish about him. Everything would have been the greatest; but not so the Bible.

The Bible tells us that one day James, this man who later gave his life for Christ, came to Jesus with John and asked a favor: "Grant unto us that we may sit, one on thy right hand, and the other on thy left hand, in thy glory" (Mark 10:37).

Here are two men; they had their mother come and say, "Grant that these my two sons may sit, the one on the right hand, and the other on the left, in thy kingdom" (Matt. 20:21). She said, "I want my two sons to be first." There were other sons, there were other mothers; but she did not care. There were other disciples, but James and John did not care! What we want is the chief seats, first place, prominence! But they didn't get it. We find that Jesus kindly rebuked them saying, 'That place is not mine to give; it is My Father's prerogative to give that unto whom He wants to give it and for whom it was prepared.' Then He turned to them and asked, 'Are ye able to be baptized with the baptism of suffering?' He was talking about suffering, dying, blood and deprivation. 'Are you able to be baptized with the baptism that I will be baptized with? That chief seat you ask for, between you and that place of prominence will come the cup of death and the cup of suffering. There will come blood and suffering for you!' (Matt. 20:22).

My friends, this desire for pre-eminence (first place) has no place in the life of a Christian. Leave that up to God. They wanted first places when He came into His kingdom.

"That in all things he might have the preeminence."—Col. 1:18.

That desire for pre-eminence caused indignation on the part of other Christians. Matthew 20:24 says, "And when the ten heard it, they were moved with indignation against the two brethren." The other ten were saying, "Why do these two think they should have first place?" This is like III John 9 where John says, "I wrote unto the church: but Diotrephes, who loveth to have the preeminence among them, receiveth us not." Even John said, 'I wrote unto the church, but there is a man in the church who desires to pervert my truth and my letter because he desires to be first.' The whole Bible rebukes this attitude. God's own nature is against it! Jesus here plainly rebuked these two who wanted first place.

This always causes trouble. More churches have been divided, more Christians have been injured because someone wanted first place or prominence or an undeserved place.

It does not, in the next place, demonstrate true Christianity. Jesus took this occasion to teach them. He says the Gentiles exercise this type of dominion and pre-eminence, but not true Christians.

"But Jesus called them unto him, and said, Ye know that the princes of the Gentiles exercise dominion over them, and they that are great exercise authority upon them. But it shall not be so among you: but whosoever will be great among you, let him be your minister; and whosoever will be chief among you, let him be your servant: even as the Son of man came not to be ministered unto, but to minister, and to give his life a ransom for many."—Matt. 20:25-28.

The giving of oneself for others is the whole heart of Christianity. Jesus said, 'Don't desire chief seats. They which would be chief among you must be servants of you all.' Here is a man who sought undeserved prominence.

May God give us that sweet spirit today that says, "I want to serve others." Then may God give us that Christlike spirit to say that He [Christ] will have all the pre-eminence. Oh, that in this church the Lord may be the pre-eminent One! I so often pray that we may see no man, save Jesus only.

James sought an undeserved prominence.

III. JAMES WAS CONCERNED WITH THE LIFE TO COME

In the third place, he was concerned with the life to come. There are not many words recorded that this great man said, but a great man he was. In Matthew 24 one day Jesus began to talk about things yet to come, things that had never happened. For instance, they looked upon that beautiful Temple that day and saw stones 45 feet long and 22 feet thick. It looked as if it could never be destroyed. Each of those huge stones weighed hundreds and hundreds of tons. Jesus said, "See ye not all these things? verily I say unto you, There shall not be left here one stone upon another, that shall not be thrown down" (vs. 2). In 70 A. D., not too many years after Jesus had died, that Temple was destroyed and those stones rolled like pebbles as destruction came. He said, 'See ye not all these things? But look to the future.'

James and John and the other disciples came privately saying, "Tell us, when shall these things be? and what shall be the sign of thy coming, and the end of the world?" (vs. 3). James was one who wanted to know when these things were going to come to pass. He was interested in things yet to come.

Christians should think of life beyond the grave. Jesus said:

"Marvel not at this: for the hour is coming in the which all that are in the graves shall hear his voice, And shall come forth; they that have done good, unto the resurrection of life; and they that have done evil, unto the resurrection of damnation."—John 5:28, 29.

Everyone in this room today is as eternal as God is. You are never going to really die. Your body will wear out someday and this little pup-tent that God put your spirit and soul in will go back to dust. But you will live forever.

Dr. Bob Jones, Sr., said that one time he was walking down a road in Florida where years ago he started Bob Jones College. As he walked along he said this great truth dawned upon him: **Bob Jones, you're going to live forever!** Somewhere beyond the grave, either in Heaven or Hell, every man is going to live forever.

James knew that. He lived for a life beyond, not this one! He was interested in the second coming of Jesus Christ. He had heard Jesus say one day:

"Let not your heart be troubled: ye believe in God, believe also in me. In my Father's house are many mansions: if it were not so, I would have told you. I go to prepare a place for you. And if I go and prepare a place for you, I will come again. . . ."— John 14:1-3.

You say to me, "How do you know that the Lord is coming?" Because He said so. He who fulfilled every promise and never broke one, said, "I will come again."

All of the disciples, including James, wanted to know when Jesus would come.

The Lord is coming. When I see the trends of humanity and the lightning-like rapidity at which things of the Bible are coming to pass and are verified, I almost feel like saying, as said John on the Isle of Patmos, "Even so, come, Lord Jesus" (Rev. 22:20).

What a happy day that will be when the Lord comes! First of all, we will have a new body. Second, there will be a reunion. We shall walk among the falling tombstones and up from the grave shall come our departed loved ones. Oh, the shouts, the happiness, the tears of joy when we clasp in our arms once again those from whom we have been separated for awhile! When He comes, we shall be made like Him.

"Beloved, now are we the sons of God, and it doth not yet appear what we shall be: but we know that, when he shall appear, we shall be like him; for we shall see him as he is. And every man that hath this hope in him purifieth himself, even as he is pure."—I John 3:2, 3.

James and others said, "We're interested in things about Your coming again and Your reign upon the earth. When shall come the end of the world?"

I am not a prophet, nor the son of a prophet, but I believe the signs of the Bible point not to the Rapture but to the Revelation when He comes WITH the church, not FOR the church. When we come to an age where human life means nothing, even the unborn life means nothing; when murder is the order of the day; when sin is rampant everywhere and those in authority seem helpless to do anything about it, I cry, "O God, how long until we will hear the trumpet blow? How long before You will come?"

James was interested in the second coming. He was interested in things beyond, when Christ shall reign a thousand years. So am I. I am looking forward to reigning with Jesus a thousand years.

IV. JAMES FORSOOK ALL TO FOLLOW JESUS

I quoted to you a while ago from Matthew 4 where James and John were with their father in the boat mending their nets when Jesus came along and called them: "Follow me, and I will make you fishers of men." A wonderful thing happened close to this in the life of James, recorded in Luke 5. One day Jesus, wanting to get away from the throng, borrowed a boat from Simon Peter. He put Himself in the boat and Simon shoved out a little from the land and Jesus began to teach the Word of God to the people. When He had finished, He said to Simon, "Let down your nets for a draught."

Simon Peter spoke up: "Master, we have toiled all night, and have taken nothing: nevertheless at thy word I will let down the net" (vs. 5). He did and he got it so full of fish that he had to call for help. James and John, Peter and Andrew were the principal figures. They unloaded the fish. Then they began to fall down at the feet of Jesus and confess their sins. We read in verse 11, "And when they had brought their ships to land, they forsook all, and followed him." They had said to Him not long before that, "Lord, we'll go where You want us to go," but they had not kept their word. This day James said, "I mean it now. I'm going to go where the Lord says go."

I wish I had time to talk on the five lessons they learned that day. First, it is impossible to live happily without Jesus. Second, it is always best to obey Him. Third, Jesus works miracles for those who obey. Fourth, they found out that day what Jesus wants most of all is for us to follow Him and be a soul winner. Fifth, they saw that their failure was because of themselves. They fell down and said, "God, be merciful to us! We are sinful men."

Have you ever forsaken all to follow Jesus? I am talking to Christians this morning. Have you disassociated yourself with everything which displeased God, in order to serve Jesus Christ?

When I was preaching in North Carolina a good many years ago, a preacher, a great man of God, told me about a young man who was saved and called to preach under his ministry. The Lord just put it on this young man's heart to serve the Lord full time. All the way for Christ

First, he must go to a Christian school and get prepared. This son of a very wealthy farmer went to his parents and said, "I know what your hope has been. You have never wanted me to leave this farm. But I'm going to be a fisherman for Jesus, not a farmer."

The parents thought their boy had had a stroke or something else had happened to him. They came to this preacher and said, "Preacher, our boy is acting strange. He told us he doesn't want this big farm, this farm worth hundreds of thousands of dollars, nor these hundreds of heads of cattle, nor all of these houses and lands. Preacher, do you suppose he's having a nervous breakdown? What's happening to him? He's talking about going to some little Christian school and that he is not going to be a farmer but a fisher of men! Could it be that our boy is going crazy?"

The preacher smiled as he answered, "No, your boy is not going crazy. God has done something in his life that is the most wonderful thing in the world to him. He wants to follow the Lord Jesus all the way." He forsook all to follow Jesus.

V. JAMES GAVE HIS LIFE FOR JESUS

I close hastily by saying this man gave his life for Jesus Christ. The Scripture says, "And he [Herod] killed James the brother of John with the sword," a fulfillment of the prophecy of Jesus. He had said to James that day when he wanted a prominent place, "Ye shall drink of my cup, and be baptized with the baptism that I am baptized with." This came to pass.

I was thinking the other day about a man giving his life for Christ, that this is a great compliment. They didn't go out and try to kill just anyone. They looked for someone who stood for something, one who was dedicated, who was a soul winner, someone who meant something to the kingdom of God. No greater compliment was ever paid a Christian than was paid to James when they decided to behead him. There is a crown in Heaven awaiting him, for the Bible says, "Be thou faithful unto death, and I will give thee a crown of life" (Rev. 2:10).

There is a wonderful story written by Clemente of Alexandria in the year 190 A. D. He was a great Christian and a great writer. He wrote the story of the surrounding events and an account of the martyrdom of James. It only had to be told through three people; like a great-grandfather who would tell it, then the grandfather would tell it, then the father would tell it. In 190 A. D. Clemente of Alexandria wrote the account of the death of James. "When they accused him of being a Christian, he said something like this: he owned up to it enthusiastically, 'Yes, I'm a Christian. Christ is all. Nothing else matters to me!' They said, 'Then we will have to kill you. You either denounce His name or die!' He said, 'I will gladly die for the One whom I love and have followed these years!' "

It is said that as his accusers stood there and with vehement words accused him, he smiled and said, "What an honor to die for Jesus Christ!" One accuser fell to his knees and said, "What faith! What love! What devotion! I, too, want to be saved." They said, "All right, you get saved and you will die, too."

James and this one accuser were led in chains toward the execution. As they led them out to the chopping block, the accuser said, "O James, will you forgive me? I accused you so vehemently and with such bitter words; will you forgive me?" Clemente of Alexandria said that James smiled back and said, "Peace be with you, my brother, I not only forgive you, but I love you." The two men then went on the chopping block, giving their lives for Christ.

I ask every man, woman, boy and girl in this room, "Would you do that?" I will tell you the way you can know whether you would or not. How much does Jesus mean to you right now? Can you come, in your own heart and soul, to an intelligent answer as to what you would do if today they said, "We are going to take your life. It is recant or die"?

James gave his life for Christ. You cannot give your life for Christ until you first give your life to Christ.

"And he [Herod] *killed James the brother of John with the sword."*

Chapter V

John, the Disciple of Love

READ: John 13:21-35.

"Now there was leaning on Jesus' bosom one of his disciples, whom Jesus loved."—Vs. 23.

"Therefore the disciple whom Jesus loved saith unto Peter, It is the Lord...."—John 21:7.

Here Jesus made probably the most startling announcement these disciples or anybody else in that day had ever heard or ever would hear. He announced that one of the twelve, one of these twelve preachers, one of these twelve apostles, one of these twelve disciples, would betray Him and deny Him—one within His own group.

When Jesus made that announcement, none of those disciples knew of whom He was speaking. They were not able to say, "Well, we all know who it is. It is Judas Iscariot." It showed the deceitfulness of sin and the hypocrisy of having religion without Christ.

Simon Peter beckoned to John, the man about whom we are preaching, and said, "...ask who it should be of whom he spake" (John 13:24). Jesus then revealed that Judas Iscariot was the one who should betray Him.

What I want to get over to you is that when you read of this disciple John, you read of a man of whom it is said three times in the Gospel of John, "he whom Jesus loved." You read of him here literally laying his head over on the bosom of the Lord Jesus Christ. So, I call him John, beloved of Jesus and John, the beloved disciple.

We need to distinguish which John this is. It is kind of like in our family. Mrs. Malone announced that we have another little Malone. There are three Toms already in our family. Tom the first, me, the old one. They said the other day that the little baby looked like me. The reason they said that is because his face was all wrinkled up. Every little baby looks a little bit like me. There is Tom, the second, and Tom, the third.

My grandfather used to get the Marys all mixed up—Mary Magdalene; Mary, the mother of Jesus, etc. One time he said, "Tom, I want you to explain to me the different Marys of the Bible."

There are three famous men in the New Testament named John. There is John the Baptist. He did not write the Gospel of John. This great wilderness preacher, clad in a camel's skin, was out in the wilderness preaching, "Repent ye: for the kingdom of heaven is at hand" (Matt. 3:2). He had thousands of people saved and baptized. John the Baptist became a martyr for his convictions.

Then a young man in the New Testament, mentioned a number of times, is named John Mark. He had a wonderful mother. The home of John Mark was a home where prayer meetings and preaching services were held. He was a missionary companion of Paul at one time, then of Barnabas later.

This John we now are discussing is called "John the Beloved." Three times he has said of himself, "he whom Jesus loved." This distinguishes him from John the Baptist and from John Mark. He was a son of Zebedee and Salome, who were wonderful parents. The word "Zebedee" means "gift." He also had a brother in the ministry named James. Salome was one of those women who loved

Jesus. She followed Him about to minister to His needs, as did other women. This John had wonderful parents.

I was thinking about the moral bankruptcy of America and of the world. The cure for that is Christian parents and Christian homes. There is no substitute for it. The whole basis for society in this country is the home, the American home. Our society is bankrupt because homes are bankrupt in the matter of morals, love and discipline. There is nothing in this world greater than a Christian man and woman with Christian leadership in the home.

He was one of three chief disciples. For many years I asked the Lord about this as I studied His Word. You know there are twelve of these disciples, and they are divided into three groups. There are three in one group, eight in one group, and one in another. Judas Iscariot is in a class by himself.

There were three that the Lord more than once showed special favoritism to. I think the Bible gives us the answer why and I will deal with that later. The three were Peter, James and John. How close they were to the Lord Jesus Christ! More than once, Jesus separated these three from the rest of the twelve and said, "Follow me."

One wonderful thing about this man John was that he wrote more. When I say wrote more, I mean God wrote through him. I believe the Bible is inspired. I do not believe that this Bible is written by men who just chose their own words and wrote what they wanted to say. I believe they were men who were absorbed and gripped by the Holy Spirit of God. God spoke through them. "...holy men of God spake as they were moved by the Holy Ghost" (II Pet. 1:21).

God spoke through this man. He wrote five books. Oh, the tremendous importance of the writings of John! The Gospel of John, three epistles of John and the greatest prophetical book in the Bible, the book of Revelation. He wrote more than all the rest put together. God laid His hand on this John we are discussing and as far as the New Testament is concerned, in writing he is second only to the Apostle Paul. God had a special work for this man to do.

John talked about four things. I could spend all the time this morning in his writings. He talked about four tremendous things. He talked about the word "belief." Ninety-nine times in the Gospel of John, he shows how to be saved. He talked about "life," about what real life is in Christ. He talked about "truth." He talked about "Heaven." Belief, life, truth and Heaven were the themes of all his writings. John was greatly used of God.

I. JOHN WAS A MAN OF FAULTS

John was a man of faults. We not only believe in the depravity of human nature—that all men are depraved and without God and without hope until they are saved—but we do not believe in what some folks talk about as sinless perfection. We believe in it, but we do not have it yet.

When you got saved, your body did not get saved. God gave you a new nature, but you still have the old. I do not need to spend much time proving that you still have the old man. When the Lord comes, we will have a new body like now we have a new spirit and we are new in Christ.

John had faults. All Christians do. I have never seen a perfect Christian. I have heard a few talk about others, like they were perfect themselves. Even the men of the Bible had feet of clay. Abraham did. Jacob did. Paul cried,

"O wretched man that I am! who shall deliver me from the body of this death?"—Rom. 7:24.

John was a man of faults. I want to mention three things that he brings out and the Bible brings out, that you might consider faults in the life of a Christian.

He was a sectarian. That is, he felt at one time, "It is our little group or it is no one." I know folks who feel that way today. For instance, Mark 9:38, "And John answered him, saying, Master, we saw one casting out devils in thy name, and he followeth not us; and we forbad him, because he followeth not us."

Now John said to Jesus, "Jesus, we saw a man in Your name, in the name of Jesus, casting out demons, ministering to people; but he wasn't with our crowd. So we forbad him to do it anymore." Jesus rebuked John. "Forbid him not...For he that is not against us is on our part" (vss. 39, 40).

I am a Baptist, and I am glad there is a man in the Bible called a John the Baptist. I have certain convictions that make me a Baptist preacher. I have definite convictions based on the Word of God that designate me as such.

I know that there are people in this world who are not called by that particular denomination who love the Lord Jesus Christ. Now I wish they were Baptists, but they are not. I must remember that I was won to Christ by a Methodist preacher. If people are saved from any denominations and are for Jesus, then I am for them.

I used to hear a great veteran of the cross say, "If a dog came to town barking for Jesus, I would say, 'Here, doggie, is a piece of bread. I want to help you.' " We need to stand with those who are standing for Jesus.

But John was sectarian. "It is us or nobody." Jesus did not condone John. Rather, He corrected him. He led him out of that feeling and that belief.

At one time in his ministry, John was a vindictive Christian. Luke 9:54, "And when his disciples James and John saw this, they said, Lord, wilt thou that we command fire to come down from heaven, and consume them, even as Elias did?" Notice this. People saw the face of Jesus set to go to Jerusalem. He was going to the cross. He came for the salvation of people. His whole life on earth pointed to that glorious hour when He would die on the cross of Calvary for the sins of the world.

As He went through the villages of the Samaritans, they saw that set face. Jesus was not grinning all the time. I like folks to sometimes look serious, like they mean business. I don't think we ought to go around smiling all the time.

When John saw Jesus' face and that it was serious, he said to Jesus, "Some folks are not receiving You because Your face is set to go to the cross. Why don't You call down fire from Heaven and destroy these people?" Jesus said, "John, away with this vindictive attitude. For the Son of man is not come to destroy men's lives, but to save them...." (Luke 9:56).

Your attitude toward God's people is important. You cannot be right with God without being right with His people. Some folks I don't enjoy being with. Some folks I am not going to fellowship with because of convictions taught in the Bible. God teaches us that we cannot have a vindictive spirit in our hearts. "Vengeance is mine; I will repay, saith the Lord" (Rom. 12:19). You had better let God settle that thing. John said, "Lord, command fire to come down and consume them." Jesus said in answer to this, "The Son of man is not come to destroy men's lives, but to save them."

Those who would destroy someone's character, someone's reputation, someone's testimony, are guilty of murder. Don't talk about the murder by abortion, the murder and homicide going on in this country today when you yourself hate people. It is godless and of the Devil. It is destructive and it grieves the Holy Spirit of God. Christians ought to be devoted to saving souls and lives.

At one time in John's life, he wanted the pre-eminence. He wanted the chief seat or none. "They said unto him, Grant unto us that we may sit, one on thy right hand, and the other on thy left hand, in thy glory" (Mark 10:37).

I never read in the New Testament where there was ever an argument among the twelve except one time. Ten were indignant against James and John, and this caused trouble in the apostolate because of what these two said: "We want the chief seats." John wanted the pre-eminence.

What people need to see today is their own need. Look at I John 1:8, "If we say that we have no sin, we deceive ourselves, and the truth is not in us." John was a man of faults.

II. JOHN WAS GREATLY FAVORED

Oh, how the Lord loved John. And John was gripped with that love. The Lord loves you today. Bless your heart, if you can realize today how God loves you, what a wonderful thing it would be.

A Presbyterian preacher from Bowling Green, Kentucky, was listening to a testimony meeting. One lady told how much she loved the Lord. When she sat down, this old Bible preacher said, "Now lady, I want to tell you something better than your love for Jesus." She looked shocked. Then he went on to say, "Something better than your love for Jesus is Jesus' love for you. Your love may change; His never will."

John was greatly favored and greatly loved.

Three times Jesus said to John, Peter and James, "I want you to come with Me." He especially favored them.

One time was when He raised a twelve-year-old girl from the dead. A man sent for Jesus and said, "My little daughter is sick." Before He could do anything about it, they brought another message, "Your daughter is dead. Don't trouble the Master anymore."

Jesus said to the man, "Fear not, only believe," and went to his home. He took Peter, James, John and the mother and dad of the twelve-year-old girl. Oh, how their hearts were broken! He takes Peter, James and John and goes into a room and closes the door. In that closed room behind a closed door, John saw something very few people ever got to see. He saw Jesus take a young girl by the hand and say unto her, ''Talitha-cumi; which is being interpreted, Damsel, I say unto thee, arise. And straightway the damsel arose and walked'' (Mark 5:41, 42).

John that day saw One who can raise the dead, One who is life Himself. Oh, how favored he was!

Friend, that is the Christ you and I walk with today—One who has power to raise the dead and bring them back to life again. What a glorious hope!

He was favored another time. One day when Jesus said, ''Verily I say unto you, That there be some of them that stand here, which shall not taste of death, till they have seen the kingdom of God come with power'' (Mark 9:1), people did not know what He was talking about.

Then He took three men, went up on a mountaintop and was transfigured. These three men, including John, saw the kingdom of God in miniature. They saw Jesus glorified as He will be when He comes. They saw two men come from Heaven who had been dead hundreds of years; one was Moses, the other, Elijah. Moses died a natural death at the age of 120 and Elijah was caught up without dying. There is the picture of all saints. Those who die in Christ, those who will remain alive until He comes. A picture of the whole church and the kingdom of God right here. John saw it all.

Another time Jesus said to John, ''John, you, Peter and James, come with Me.'' I wish you could see that moment, that hour. It was the night of His arrest. The next day He will hang on the cross between two thieves, dying for the sins of the world. But that night, east of the city, He came out of the Upper Room, down across the little brook Kedron and out on the side of the slope of the Mount of Olives, to the Garden of Gethsemane. Eleven men followed Him, Judas having already denied Him.

He enters that garden and that night in the garden He is to pray until great drops of blood ooze from the pores of His skin and drop down into a crimson pool in the moonlight. That night He said to three men, "Peter, James and John, come with Me." He went a little farther. He left eight at the gate and led three into the heart of the garden.

They heard Him cry, "Father, all things are possible unto thee, take away this cup from me: nevertheless not what I will, but what thou wilt" (Mark 14:36). They saw the blood, the crimson stream run down His face as His soul almost broke through His body. John saw all that.

Why? Why was he favored of God?

He was to write of the coming kingdom of God. I want to say something to you; with privilege comes responsibility. I used to and still do pray, "O God, use my life." Nothing on earth would mean as much to me as having God use me. I did not know when I was a young man and prayed to be used of God that with privilege comes great responsibility and sometimes great suffering.

God never uses any Christian unless at some time He puts that Christian's soul upon the anvil of His sovereign dealing and chastises and deals with that life.

Jesus knew that one day out yonder on a little rocky isle called Patmos, John would be separated from the world, persecuted and would suffer. He wanted John to remember, "I was with Him in intimacy three times. Behind a closed door I saw Him raise the dead. I was with Him that day on the mountain when God from Heaven spoke, 'This is my beloved Son in whom I am well pleased, hear ye him.'" He wanted John to remember, "I was with Him that night when He prayed and sweat drops of blood." So out on that little rocky island, John could pray, "I care not what happens to me. Not my will, but Thine be done." He favored

John because He wanted John to always know He was God manifest in the flesh.

I know of a fine Christian man who lives in another city, but he loves this work and helps this college and this church. Years ago he and his dear wife, before they ever knew how God would bless them materially, adopted a boy. I have been with that man several times. I am never with him but what he tells of his love for that boy, his provision for that boy, his care for that boy. I never think of it but what I think one day the King of Heaven adopted me into His family. I am an heir with God, a joint heir with Jesus Christ. He has blessed me with all spiritual blessings in the heavenlies. I am a child of the King!

John was favored of the Lord, and so are you. And so am I. We are in Christ.

III. JOHN WAS FULL OF LOVE

John loved Jesus and was loved by Jesus.

"Behold, what manner of love the Father hath bestowed upon us, that we should be called the sons of God: therefore the world knoweth us not, because it knew him not. Beloved, now are we the sons of God, and it doth not yet appear what we shall be: but we know that, when he shall appear, we shall be like him; for we shall see him as he is."—I John 3:1, 2.

John talked about loving other people. "If a man say, I love God, and hateth his brother, he is a liar: for he that loveth not his brother whom he hath seen, how can he love God whom he hath not seen?" (I John 4:20). He was literally full of love for others. He had heard Jesus as He spoke in John 13 the night of His betrayal, "By this shall all men know that ye are my disciples, if ye have love one to another" (vs. 35).

John loved the truth. He talked about the truth. "And ye shall know the truth, and the truth shall make you free" (John 8:32).

"I have no greater joy than to hear that my children walk in truth" (III John 4).

The other day I had occasion to listen to a man whose pastor is a great man of God. Talking to my wife and me, this man said, "You know, some folks ask me what makes this man great. I always tell them that he loves people who have and he loves people who don't have."

That is God's will for every one of us. It is wonderful to know what God can do in your life to make you full of love.

John was full of love. He loved Jesus, he loved others, and he loved the truth.

IV. HE FORSOOK ALL TO FOLLOW JESUS

The Bible says when they got to land, they forsook all and followed Him.

"And going on from thence, he saw other two brethren, James the son of Zebedee, and John his brother, in a ship with Zebedee their father, mending their nets; and he called them. And they immediately left the ship and their father, and followed him."—Matt. 4:21, 22.

"And when they had brought their ships to land, they forsook all, and followed him."—Luke 5:11.

Jesus gives this great challenge more than once in His great teaching and ministry. He said in Mark 8:34, "And when he had called the people unto him with his disciples also, he said unto them, Whosoever will come after me, let him deny himself, and take up his cross, and follow me."

I get three things out of that tremendous verse. First, what the Christian's attitude is to be toward self. "If any man would come after me," Jesus said, "let him deny himself." No matter how you look at it or interpret it, you cannot be a good Christian without self-denial!

I know the Lord has promised to meet our needs. God is not an enemy to having our physical needs met. The Bible teaches that a Christian cannot live as he pleases; he must live a life of self-denial. "If any man come after me, let him deny himself." I learned that what God's Word teaches is the attitude of a Christian toward himself: denying self.

I learned, secondly, what a Christian's attitude is to be toward Jesus Christ. "If any man come after me, let him deny himself and take up his cross and follow me."

I learned what his attitude is to be toward the world. A Christian is going to choose either one of two things: either the cross or the world. Paul said in Galatians 6:14, "But God forbid that I should glory, save in the cross of our Lord Jesus Christ, by whom the world is crucified unto me, and I unto the world."

Which have you chosen, the cross or the world? Every Christian must make that choice. "If any man come after me, let him take up his cross and follow me."

The other night while sitting in a room in Lynchburg, Virginia, waiting for the service to start, I saw a little man walk in. He was without arms and legs, yet in motivation. He came into the room walking with artificial limbs. He had a smile on his face as he entered. He walked in like he owned the world!

The preacher said to me, "That young man is a saved Jew. His parents said, 'You no longer will live in this home, even though you are without arms and legs.' This young man said, 'I found Christ, and I will follow Him, no matter what it costs.' He gave up his home and all else. He gave up financial security to follow Jesus Christ."

A little later on at the service, a very famous singer said, "I want someone to sing with me." Here comes this little converted Jew, a very handsome fellow, with no arms or legs, just two hooks, to the microphone. He held it with a smile on his countenance that only God put there. He sang of his love for Jesus Christ. John said, "I will follow Jesus the rest of my life."

V. JOHN WAS A MAN OF PRAYER AND HOLINESS

You have to read more than just the Gospel of John to get the whole picture of his life. In the book of Acts we see Peter and John being a great team for much of their ministry. Acts 3 is the record of the first great miracle wrought after Pentecost, the healing of the lame man.

"Now Peter and John went up together into the temple at the hour of prayer, being the ninth hour. And a certain man lame from his mother's womb was carried, whom they laid daily at the gate of the temple which is called Beautiful, to ask alms of them that entered into the temple."—Vss. 1, 2.

"And he took him by the right hand, and lifted him up: and immediately his feet and ankle bones received strength."—Vs. 7.

One day there came two men at the hour of prayer into the house of God. "Now Peter and John went up together into the temple at the hour of prayer, being the ninth hour" (Acts 3:1). They said, "It is time to pray." Christians ought to be in God's house engaged in prayer.

The longer I live and try to walk with my Lord and the longer I study His Word, the more I realize what a miracle it is when a Christian learns to walk with God. Oh, how his life changes when a Christian learns to walk with God in the secret place of prayer.

John was a man of prayer and a man of boldness and holiness. Now when they saw the boldness of Peter and John and how they healed the lame man, they were hated for it. Mark it down, that a Christian will be hated for doing good. Go out and get drunk; no one is going to hate you. They will laugh and say, "So-and-so, trying to be a Christian, went out and got drunk.'' But you get to winning souls and you will be a separated Christian. You start following the Lord and those of the world will not laugh but hate you. Jesus said so. ''If the world hate you, ye know that it hated me before it hated you'' (John 15:18).

''Now when they saw the boldness of Peter and John, and perceived that they were unlearned and ignorant men, they marvelled; and they took knowledge of them that they had been with Jesus.''—Acts 4:13.

This world is against a Christian. And that is why a Christian ought to come out from the world. Be separated. Have no part of it, except to love and win people to Christ.

When they saw the boldness of Peter and John after having gotten this man healed, then all hell broke loose. They imprisoned them, threatened them, and inquired how they did this. Simon Peter said, ''It was wrought in the name of Jesus whom you crucified, who now is raised from the dead. By His name this man stands here before you, whole.''

That did not go over very well. They were put in prison. But ''when they saw the boldness of Peter and John...they [the Sanhedrin] marvelled; and they took knowledge of them.'' Peter and John were not learned; they had no theological degree, but, 'these men have been with Jesus.' That is what people ought to be able to say of every Christian.

John was a man of prayer, holiness and power. John had been taught by Jesus to pray. He heard Jesus say, when He preached that tremendous Sermon on the Mount, how men when they pray, like to be heard of men. ''But thou, when thou prayest, enter into thy closet, and when thou hast shut thy door, pray to thy Father which is in secret; and thy Father which seeth in secret shall reward thee openly'' (Matt. 6:6). Jesus had taught them to pray. ''And all things, whatsoever ye shall ask in prayer, believing, ye shall receive'' (Matt. 21:22). John recognized that all power came from God.

"Be it known unto you all, and to all the people of Israel, that by the name of Jesus Christ of Nazareth, whom ye crucified, whom God raised from the dead, even by him doth this man stand here before you whole'' (Acts 4:10). He had a testimony that could be seen. My dear Christian friends, the only kind of testimony worth anything is the testimony that can be seen.

"Now when they saw the boldness of Peter and John, and perceived that they were unlearned and ignorant men [that is by the world's standards], they marvelled; and they took knowledge of them, that they had been with Jesus.'' They saw their testimony.

That ought to be true of any Christian. Tell your friends, neighbors and associates that you love the Lord, but let them see it.

That is the kind of Christianity and power of God that John had. When people think of God's power, they should be able to say, "Our pastor has it.'' Preachers ought to have it, but every Christian ought to have a testimonial power of God visible to the outsider and others. Are others able to see that unusual power of God in your life?

I heard a friend of mine tell of some highly educated engineers who were trying to get a large column out of the ocean where there had been a causeway or bridge. They tried everything. They hooked a big cable on it and got on land to pull it but it wouldn't budge. They put a big crane on a large barge and divers went down and hooked cables onto the bottom of it. The barge nearly turned over, yet they could not move the column.

Finally, a man came along and said, "I believe I can get that out of there for you.'' He was not a great engineer but he knew something. This man got about four of these barges and surrounded the column, went down and hooked onto its base that would not move by any power that man had.

They said, "We're hooked onto it; now what?"

"Move it! I think in a little while it will come out of there."

They laughed and said, "It is not coming out of there!"

He said, "Yes, I think it will." He had hooked onto it while the tide was low, and when the tide came in, God sent the power in! Those barges began to creak as they began to lift, and that column jumped from the water like it was literally shot from the deep.

In astonishment, the highly educated engineers asked, "How did this happen?"

He said, "God's power is in this ocean, and we merely harnessed onto this wonderful power." Let me say to you, everyone should be harnessed to the wonderful power of God. That is what John had.

VI. JOHN KNEW HE WAS SAVED AND WHY

He was a wonderful man of prayer and of a holy life. John knew he was saved and he knew why.

I know of nothing more important than this. Just a few days ago a group of Bible college students were asked, "How many of you are justified?" Someone told me not everybody in that group could say, "Yes, I know I am justified."

John knew he was saved, and he knew why he was saved.

There is a beautiful relationship between the Gospel of John and the Epistles of John. He tells why both of these were written: "But these are written, that ye might believe that Jesus is the Christ, the Son of God; and that believing ye might have life through his name" (John 20:31). John said it was written that you might believe that Jesus is the Son of God.

The Gospel that distinctly sets Christ as King is Matthew; as Servant in Mark; Luke sets Him apart as the Son of man; John sets Him forth as He who came from Heaven. God with us and tabernacled in human flesh. It exalts Him as the Son of God.

"These things have I written unto you that believe on the name of the Son of God; that ye may know that ye have eternal life, and that ye may believe on the name of the Son of God" (I John 5:13).

If someone asked you if you are a Christian, you ought to be able to definitely say, "Yes, I am."

"Do you know you are saved?"

You ought to be able to say, "I know I am saved," with the same confidence that you could say, "I know I am sitting in this church."

Do you know you are saved? Some say, "I don't know how to know why I am saved and know that I am saved." Most go about this the wrong way. They do the traditional things and say, "Sometimes I feel like I am saved, and sometimes I don't feel like I am."

Sometimes that is the way I feel when I have a headache and I am tired, but I would not go on that feeling for anything in the world. I know I am still saved.

You ask, "How do you know that you are saved?"

Because the Bible tells me I am. You must believe that He is divine.

"For many deceivers are entered into the world, who confess not that Jesus Christ is come in the flesh. This is a deceiver and an antichrist. Look to yourselves, that we lose not those things which we have wrought, but that we receive a full reward. Whosoever transgresseth, and abideth not in the doctrine of Christ, hath not God. He that abideth in the doctrine of Christ, he hath both the Father and the Son. If there come any unto you, and bring not this doctrine, receive him not into your house, neither bid him God speed: For he that biddeth him God speed is partaker of his evil deeds."—II John 7-11.

You must by faith believe in Him.

"And as Moses lifted up the serpent in the wilderness, even so must the Son of man be lifted up: That whosoever believeth in him should not perish, but have eternal life. For God so loved the world, that he gave his only begotten Son, that whosoever believeth in him should not perish, but have everlasting life."—John 3:14-16.

"Verily, verily, I say unto you, He that heareth my word, and believeth on him that sent me, hath everlasting life, and shall not come into condemnation; but is passed from death unto life."— John 5:24.

God said it! You can know you are saved.

Feeling has absolutely nothing to do with it. Sometimes you say, "I do not act like a Christian." True; but if you believe in Jesus Christ, the Son of God, as your Saviour, you have eternal life.

Suppose someone comes to me and says, "Do you know who that car belongs to?"

I say, "It belongs to me."

Suppose he says, "Prove that it belongs to you."

I say, "I bought that car from the showroom and no one else has owned it." That does not prove a thing in the world.

I say, "I saved to make payments on that car once a month. I know it is mine because I paid for it." That does not mean a thing in the world.

I say, "But it has four wheels and an engine. It is a red car and it is my car." But here comes another red car with four wheels.

I know that car is mine because I can produce the title that gives the motor and vehicle numbers, description, registration and name.

I know I am saved because the Bible says so. "These things have I written unto you that believe...that ye may know that ye have eternal life...."

John was saved and he knew that he was. He was a man of tremendous assurance and wrote about it much of the time.

VII. JOHN KNEW WHAT THE FUTURE HELD FOR HIM

God revealed much of the prophetic truths to John. Three things I want to mention.

He saw Christ as his living Lord and Advocate. One day they said to John, "Because of your testimony, you are going to be put on a rocky isle called Patmos."

Some years ago we were flying over that part of the sea when the pilot said on the intercom, "Down there on a lovely day one can easily see the Isle of Patmos." We looked out the window and there was that little barren, rocky isle.

As we were flying thousands of feet in the air, I thought of John being the only person on that island. He had been placed in exile there. One day the Lord spoke to John from Heaven: "I am he that liveth, and was dead: and, behold, I am alive for evermore, Amen; and have the keys of hell and of death" (Rev. 1:18). John saw a living Lord. That is what I have. This is what every Christian has. Our Lord lives on His throne and mediates our cause. We are not alone. We have a Lawyer in the Glory. He never slumbers or sleeps but keeps our slate clear every moment of the day and night.

John saw something else. He saw Christ as his coming King. When John came to the close of the book of Revelation, the unveiling of Jesus, he wrote of the second coming of Christ with such beautiful clarity: "Behold, I come quickly: blessed is he that keepeth the sayings of the prophecy of this book" (Rev. 22:7). "And, behold, I come quickly; and my reward is with me, to give every man according as his work shall be" (Rev. 22:12).

I think of this verse when I see some of our people drive a bus out here, call and knock on the doors of people that no one else cares about. Our people care. The day will come when the Lord will say, "Well done, thou good and faithful bus driver." The day will come when the Lord will say, "God bless you for teaching that class, for winning those boys and girls to Christ." When rewards are given out, it will be to those who have served Him faithfully.

I heard the song here last Wednesday night, "Must I go and empty-handed be?" Perish the thought that we go before Him empty-handed, He whose hands held the cross!

John saw his Christ as his coming King. "He which testifieth these things saith, Surely I come quickly. Amen" (Rev. 22:20).

I guess John was tired of that old rocky island, so he said, "Lord, I would like for You to come. I would like to exchange this old rocky island for a home with my Saviour. Even so, come, Lord Jesus."

That is the desire of my life. I want to see Jesus. Thirty-eight years ago He walked across the threshold of my life. He changed me and made me a new creature, blotted out my transgressions and put them behind His back, to be remembered no more forever. He washed me in His blood as clean as if I had never sinned. Thirty-eight years He has walked with me through sunshine, through shadows and joy and sorrow, never failing me one time. I want to reign with Him a thousand years and kiss His feet and thank Him for saving a sinner like me.

John saw Heaven as his eternal home.

"And I saw a new heaven and a new earth; for the first heaven and the first earth were passed away; and there was no more sea. And I John saw the holy city, new Jerusalem, coming down from God out of heaven, prepared as a bride adorned for her husband."—Rev. 21:1, 2.

John said, "I see the city—there is no night there, no pain or sin there, no sorrow or tears there, for He wipes them away."

John saw Heaven as his eternal home.

"And I heard a great voice out of heaven saying, Behold, the tabernacle of God is with men, and he will dwell with them, and they shall be his people, and God himself shall be with them, and be their God. And God shall wipe away all tears from their eyes; and there shall be no more death, neither sorrow, nor crying, neither shall there be any more pain: for the former things are passed away."—Vss. 3, 4.

Thank God for the hope of Heaven!

We had in our church a little lady who loved the Lord. One day after her return from the hospital, sitting in her home she bowed her head and said, "Thank You, Lord, for saving my soul and my family. Thank You for the food. Thank You for a home in Heaven. Amen." She never lifted her head but just went on out into eternity.

My friends, that hope cannot be bought with all the money in the world! We have been purchased by His precious blood on the cross.

John saw Heaven as his eternal home.

"Now there was leaning on Jesus' bosom one of his disciples, whom Jesus loved."—John 13:23.

"Therefore the disciple whom Jesus loved saith unto Peter, It is the Lord...."—John 21:7.

Chapter VI

Philip—the Man Who Walked by Sight

READ: John 1:35-51.

"The day following Jesus would go forth into Galilee, and findeth Philip, and saith unto him, Follow me."—John 1:43.

Philip is mentioned only three times in Matthew, Mark and Luke. Keep in mind that the Holy Spirit of God wrote the Bible. The three times Philip is mentioned is in a list of the twelve disciples in Matthew, Mark and Luke.

But in the Gospel of John it seems the Holy Spirit of God stands this great man out in front of us and gives us a character study of this member of the twelve.

He was from Bethsaida. That word means "the place of nets"— fishing nets. It was the home town of two other famous Christians, Peter and Andrew. Philip was from the same town as these two fisherman brothers whom the Lord saved and called.

There were two Bethsaidas. One on the east side and one on the west bank of the Sea of Galilee. This is the Bethsaida on the west bank. Around the shores of the Sea of Galilee Jesus ministered a great deal of the time.

This is the Bethsaida Jesus referred to when He said,

" Then began he to upbraid the cities wherein most of his mighty

works were done, because they repented not: Woe unto thee,
Chorazin! woe unto thee, Bethsaida! for if the mighty works, which
were done in you, had been done in Tyre and Sidon, they would
have repented long ago in sackcloth and ashes.''—Matt. 11:20, 21.

Here is what the Lord was saying: ''Woe unto you, Bethsaida.
If the works that have been done in you had been done in those
Phoenician cities, Tyre and Sidon, they would have repented, but
you haven't repented.''

Here is a city that had seen the mighty works of God, yet had
not repented. But one day the grace of God reached down in the
wicked city and God put His hand upon a man's life by the name
of Philip.

That means something to me. There are wicked cities all over
the world. Wickedness is everywhere. The environment of the earth
is a depraved one. But God, out of that environment, is able to
lay hold of men's lives, change them and save them. That is what
He did here. In Bethsaida, a city that wanted no part of God, the
Lord laid His hands upon a man.

''The day following Jesus would go forth into Galilee, and findeth
Philip, and saith unto him, Follow me.''

I. HE WAS GENUINELY SAVED

Philip was genuinely saved. When the Lord came to Philip, He
said, ''Philip, follow Me.'' If you will study the Scriptures, you
will see that Philip did exactly that. The challenge of Christianity, the challenge of the Lord Jesus is saying to people, ''Follow
me.'' That is what He said to Philip.

I said that if you will study the Scriptures, you will find that
Philip did follow the Lord. Read John 8:12: ''Then spake Jesus
again unto them, saying, I am the light of the world: he that
followeth me shall not walk in darkness.'' You only have one of

two choices: to either follow Him in faith, believing, or walk in darkness.

Philip gave this tremendous testimony. He went to Nathanael and to others and said, "We have found him of whom Moses in the law, and the prophets, did write." He is the one I too have found. There is no other. Jesus said in John 5:39, "Search the scriptures; for in them ye think ye have eternal life: and they are they which testify of me."

I am saying this because people want to humanize Jesus. There are two great mass movements in the world today.

One is to deify man. First, they say, "There is not much wrong with man anyhow. He has a spark of divinity in him; with a little fanning that spark of divinity will blaze up." Listen, you can fan yourself to death and it will not work that way! Man has no divinity in him. Man is depraved.

The other is to humanize Jesus; to bring Him down to a human level. They say, "He had an earthly father like everyone else. He was born the natural way, the human way, like everybody else." That is not what the Word of God says. He was born without an earthly father—virgin-born, and He is God. I don't want a lesser Jesus. I want Jesus just like He is. I do not want Him humanized. He is God, so you cannot humanize Him. He is the Son of God.

Philip had a personal testimony. If you are saved, you too have one. I do not believe in this "lockjaw" kind of religion where people say, "I am a Christian, but I don't believe in acting the fool about it." I do not believe in acting the fool about it either, but the Bible says, "For the scripture saith, Whosoever believeth on him shall not be ashamed" (Rom. 10:11). Philip had a testimony.

Some time ago a man came out to this church. He still comes here. He got saved here. He was a lost sinner and a drunkard and everything that a man ought not to be. He came to this church, heard the Word of God and the Lord saved him.

Some churches do not try to win anybody. They sit around and wait for them to get saved somewhere else, then they light into them and try to get them to come to their church. They do not go out and knock on doors, shake the bushes, and weep over people. But let one of them get saved, then they want to get hold of them.

This is what they did to this man. They said, "You don't want to go to that Emmanuel Baptist Church." They gave him the old routine. You have heard it a thousand times and I have too. I have gotten to the point where I enjoy it, really. They said, "All they talk about out there is money; the preacher gets it all. He is a dictator there."

Do you know what the new Christian said? "Well, I will tell you this much: I found the Lord there. The place where I can find the Lord is all right with me."

II. PHILIP WAS GREATLY CONCERNED

Here is a man with a concern for others. He was not one who merely believed, "Now I am saved. If a person wants to get saved, let him get saved. Let every man root for himself." That is not Christianity. Philip was greatly concerned. He said to Nathanael, "We have found him," because he was interested in getting him saved. He had a love for others. Without love there is no Christianity. Christianity is loving people. Philip loved Nathanael and wanted him saved.

I like what he said to him. I get thrilled every time I read it. Nathanael said to Philip, "Jesus came from Nazareth, the most wicked town there ever was." It is wicked. It is probably one of the most unfriendly places you will go in the Bible lands today. Nathanael said, "Can any good thing come out of Nazareth?" I like what Philip replied: "Come and see." He did not say, "Let me give you a lecture on theology." He said only, "Just come try it. Try Jesus." I will say that to you: Try Jesus. If you try Him, you will find He is the dearest Friend any human being can ever have.

Somebody was talking one time to a caretaker at a church in the South where one of my friends is pastor. One day this salesman came in. The caretaker asked, "Have you been born again?"

The salesman said, "Why, there is nothing to all that business of being born again."

This caretaker said, "Now, you shouldn't have said that."

"What should I have said?" the salesman asked.

"You should have said, 'As far as I know, there is nothing to it.' Because you don't know. You haven't tried it," replied the caretaker.

I have tried it and I have found there is something to believing in Jesus.

Philip was concerned for others. Jesus said to Nathanael, "Before that Philip called thee, when thou wast under the fig tree, I saw thee" (John 1:48). I lay hold on that little expression: "Philip called thee." Philip was out there calling Nathanael, reaching out to Nathanael. Philip said, "He has saved me and He has put love in my heart. I want to get somebody else saved." Philip was greatly concerned for other people.

Paul, too, was concerned.

"I say the truth in Christ, I lie not, my conscience also bearing me witness in the Holy Ghost, That I have great heaviness and continual sorrow in my heart. For I could wish that myself were accursed from Christ for my brethren, my kinsmen according to the flesh."—Rom. 9:1-3.

A friend of mine went down in the islands, in the Caribbean area. He met a missionary there who was eighty years old. This missionary had been there preaching the Word of God, getting people saved, ill of health and operating his ministry on a very minimum amount of support, suffering and paying a price. My friend said, "You know, I felt sorry for him. I really pitied him and began to talk to him. When that fellow saw what I was doing and heard what I was saying, he said to me, 'Now wait just a minute. Forget the cost—on with the Gospel! I don't care what it costs me to get somebody saved.' " People were being saved by the hundreds. That ought to be the attitude of every Christian.

How much interest do you have in souls—not just you and yours, but every man, woman, boy and girl around the world?

III. PHILIP WAS GRACIOUSLY TESTED

When I say Philip was graciously tested, I mean the Lord very tenderly and graciously tested his faith. All that you learn in the Gospel of John. In John 6 is the greatest public miracle Jesus ever wrought. It involved more people and it is told in all four of the Gospels. That is not true of any other miracle.

It was the feeding of the five thousand, besides perhaps ten or twelve thousand others. There is no telling how many people the Lord fed that day. He was sitting upon a mountain and as He looked down and saw this vast multitude, He turned to Philip and said, "Whence shall we buy bread, that these may eat?" (vs. 5). How would you like to be asked that question? Maybe there are fifteen or eighteen thousand people and someone says to you, "How are we going to get enough bread for all these to eat?"

Philip looked at the crowd. He knew his faith was being tested. The next verse says Jesus already knew what He was going to do, but He asked this to prove Philip. Philip says, "Two hundred pennyworth of bread is not sufficient for them, that every one of them may take a little" (vs. 7). His faith was not really strong. What Philip was saying is, "I don't know how we are going to do it."

God tests the faith of His people. It is a test of faith today to still believe that the Bible is true and Christ is able to save from sin. The very nature of faith almost demands that it be tested. The definition of faith demands that it be tested, "Now faith is the substance of things hoped for, the evidence of things not seen" (Heb. 11:1). The expression "not seen" would suggest that our faith will be tested. "For we walk by faith, not by sight" (II Cor. 5:7).

He tested Philip's faith, then wrought this mighty miracle. I like the results. Everybody was fed and twelve baskets full were left over. I would have liked to have seen those twelve disciples going home, each with a big basket over his shoulder! I imagine each thought, *Well, I will never doubt Him again. I now know what He can do!*

"The day following Jesus would go forth into Galilee, and findeth Philip, and saith unto him, Follow me."

IV. HE WAS GLORIOUSLY TAUGHT

In John 14 is a beautiful picture. In John 13 Jesus is in the Upper Room and there is the institution of the Lord's Supper in that room. Judas has already betrayed Him at the Supper. They sing a hymn and Jesus walks out and starts toward the Garden of Gethsemane, where He will be arrested and where He will sweat great drops of blood.

He starts from the Upper Room to the garden, talking as He goes:

"Let not your heart be troubled: ye believe in God, believe also in me. In my Father's house are many mansions: if it were not so, I would have told you. I go to prepare a place for you. And if I go and prepare a place for you, I will come again, and receive you unto myself; that where I am, there ye may be also. And whither I go ye know, and the way ye know. Thomas saith unto him, Lord, we know not whither thou goest; and how can we know the way?

Jesus saith unto him, I am the way, the truth, and the life: no man cometh unto the Father, but by me. If ye had known me, ye should have known my Father also: and from henceforth ye know him, and have seen him. Philip saith unto him, Lord, shew us the Father, and it sufficeth us.''—John 14:1-8.

Philip said, ''All we want is to know the One true God, the Father. Show us the Father.''

The Bible shows us that some men in various times wanted to see God. Philip too said, ''I would like to see the Father.'' I would, too. Wouldn't you?

Job said, ''For I know that my redeemer liveth, and that he shall stand at the latter day upon the earth: And though after my skin worms destroy this body, yet in my flesh shall I see God'' (Job 19:25, 26). What meant more to Job than anything was to ''see God.''

Moses said to God one time, ''I want to see Your glory.'' God answered Moses, ''If you did, it would kill you. I will put you in the cleft of the rock, then I will pass by and you will see My hindmost glory—just a glimpse of it.'' Moses longed to see God.

John 1:18, ''No man hath seen God at any time.'' But we see Him in Christ Jesus.

I have not seen the Father, but I met Jesus Christ in 1935. I met Him who is one with the Father. I met Him who said, ''He that hath seen me hath seen the Father.'' I am glad God is my Father. Jesus said, ''I and my Father are one'' (John 10:30). That being true, if you by faith have seen the Lord Jesus Christ, you have seen the Father. They are one!

I read years ago of a little lad whose dad was a lost, wicked man. One Sunday morning the father put a dollar bill in his son's hand and sent him to the store with a note to the groceryman for some items, including some beer.

The little boy started out on that wintry, cold morning gripping that dollar bill. But the wind blew it out of his hand. It frightened him to death. He had been beaten before by his father. That morning he just stepped back in the doorway of the store and cried.

A godly man came by on his way to church. When he saw the little boy in the doorway crying, he stepped up to him, put his hand on him and asked, "Son, why do you cry?"

The little lad replied, "My father is so cruel. He gave me a dollar and sent me to the store. He drinks. I lost the dollar. I am afraid to go home. I am afraid he will kill me."

That good man told him about Jesus. He told him about One who loved him and who could save him. Then he reached in his pocket and took out a dollar bill and folded it in the lad's hand and said, "Now, son, I do not believe in this drinking business, but I love you and I do not want you hurt. Take this dollar and get what he sent you after, then go home and don't be afraid. Jesus will go with you now."

It is said that where the tears had streamed down his little face it had made some clean lines. He lifted his tear-stained face up to that man and said, "Sir, I wish you were my father."

You know, there was a time in my life when I lifted my heart toward the perfect One and said, "O God, I wish You were my Father." That day, I became a child of God.

V. PHILIP WAS GRASPING FOR FACTS

Philip said, "Show me the facts before I believe." That is the kind of man he was. He said, "Two hundred pennyworth of bread is not sufficient for them" (John 6:7). And II Corinthians 5:7 says, "For we walk by faith, not by sight." Philip wanted to walk by sight and not by faith. He said, "I want to see; show me the facts and I will believe."

In a way, there is nothing wrong with that. The fact of the Word of God is the basis of our faith. There is the truth, the living truth.

On the facts of God's Word we base our faith. But Philip wanted to walk by sight, not by faith.

Friends, there is only one way to be saved. It is not by sight, nor by feeling, nor by doing, nor by religion; it is by believing on Jesus Christ. There must be a step in that direction on the part of every individual when you take the step of faith, not by sight, but by faith.

Years ago in a big drought out in the West, water was at a minimum. Cattle were about to die. Every rancher was trying to save his herd and preserve every drop of water during that drought. It is said that when the cattle would wade out into the little watering holes, much of the water became wasted and unusable. It is said that one cattleman devised a special drinking trough. It was built out of wood, of course, and floated upon the little water holes. The only way that an animal could drink out of it was to step out on it. The weight of the animal would push it down, and in a special area of the trough the water would come up and the animal would drink.

It is said that the animals gathered around the watering hole and they looked at this strange thing, something unknown to them. They would not go out on it. They stood around it and literally begged for water.

Finally one of the herd began to walk out on this special-made trough. When he put his weight on it, the water came up and he began to drink. When he did that the other cattle began to climb over one another to walk out on this wooden trough in order to drink. Their weight brought it into reality. "O taste and see that the Lord is good: blessed is the man that trusteth in him" (Ps. 34:8).

That is the way it is with being saved. The Bible not only says to believe IN Him; it says to believe ON Him, that is, put the weight of your soul on Jesus Christ. That is what Philip did. And that is what God wants you to do. Cast your soul upon the mercy of the Lord Jesus Christ today.

"The day following Jesus would go forth into Galilee, and findeth Philip, and saith unto him, Follow me."—John 1:43.

Chapter VII

Nathanael, the Skeptic

READ: John 1:44-51.

"Nathanael answered and saith unto him, Rabbi, thou art the Son of God. . . ."

"Nathanael" means "the gift of God." This has great significance about this man who came to know the Lord Jesus Christ.

He was a skeptic. A skeptic is one who says, "I cannot believe that." He wants to rationalize and only believe what he knows in his mind but he does not accept the matter of faith. Nathanael was a skeptic. When Philip came to Nathanael and said, "We have found him," Nathanael did not believe that. There was the greatest statement a person could ever hear. I know the greatest thing that ever happened in my life was when I found Jesus and Jesus found me. That is true of you, if you are a Christian. Philip was proud of that and he came saying to Nathanael, "We have found him" (vs. 45).

Nathanael answered and said, "Can there any good thing come out of Nazareth?" (vs. 46). He said, "Up there at Nazareth, that wicked city—you mean one has come out of Nazareth who is a Saviour?" Nathanael was a skeptic. The Lord can save a person with a skeptical mind, as He did Nathanael.

His name means "the gift of God." I do not know of anything

that needs to be made more clear to people today than this: that salvation IS the gift of God. Jesus plainly taught that. You do not earn salvation; you cannot buy it and no one deserves it. It is a gift of God. Constantly the Bible teaches that salvation is the gift of God.

Remember the conversation of Jesus with the woman at the well? Jesus said, "Give me to drink," and engaged her in conversation. Then He said to her, "If thou knewest the gift of God, and who it is that saith to thee, Give me to drink; thou wouldest have asked of him, and he would have given thee living water" (John 4:10).

Jesus said, "If you knew the gift of God"—the gift being Jesus Christ. You see that taught in the Bible. Romans 6:23, "For the wages of sin is death; but the gift of God is eternal life through Jesus Christ our Lord." There are so many religions today where the whole thing is based on man earning his way into the kingdom of God. Earning your salvation is not taught in the Bible. Salvation is clearly defined as being the gift of God. You do not pay for a gift, and salvation is a gift. "For by grace are ye saved through faith; and that not of yourselves: it is the gift of God: Not of works, lest any man should boast" (Eph. 2:8, 9).

There are going to be millions in Heaven, but multiplied millions of religious people will never get to Heaven. But one thing we will never hear there is somebody boasting of how he got there. No one in Heaven ever will. No one in Heaven will ever take the glory to themselves. No one in Heaven will ever say, "I got here by my own merits, through my good works. I earned a place in Heaven." No one in Heaven will ever say that, for salvation is the gift of God, not of works lest any man should boast. No person in Heaven will ever boast about being there or about how he got there, because everybody who gets to Heaven is going to accept the free gift of God.

This man Nathanael was gloriously saved and greatly used, though seldom mentioned. Only ten verses in all the four Gospels even bear his name. Around him is a world of great Bible truth. I would like for you to see some of it in this message about Nathanael.

I. HE WAS DIVINELY CHOSEN

First of all, Nathanael was divinely chosen by Jesus Christ. This opens up a whole world of truth. Here was a skeptic; but one day the Lord came into his life and He chose this man. How thrilling, because I can apply that wonderful truth to my own life and to every Christian. Oh, how the Bible beautifully teaches that we are chosen in Christ! For instance, look at John 6:70: "Jesus answered them, Have not I chosen you twelve...." Now you and I would not have chosen the ones He chose. But, in His divine sovereignty and omniscience, Jesus chose these particular twelve.

To a man who asked, "Can any good thing come out of Nazareth?" Jesus said, "I am choosing you." That is what happened to everyone who is saved. You were divinely chosen. That makes a great difference in my thinking about what it means to be a Christian. John 15:16 declares, "Ye have not chosen me, but I have chosen you, and ordained you, that ye should go and bring forth fruit, and that your fruit should remain...." Jesus said that.

We talk about a person being saved, or maybe give our own testimony and say we have found the Lord. That is what Philip said when he came to Nathanael. You know, there is a greater truth than our finding Him, and that is, the Lord has found us. You are not sitting there a Christian by coincidence or by accident, but by the divine providence of God. You have been chosen in Christ. "According as he hath chosen us in him before the foundation of the world, that we should be holy and without blame before him in love'' (Eph. 1:4). Think of it. Before the Lord ever made a world, He looked down and said,''I am choosing Tom Malone.'' An importance and emphasis is given to a Christian's life by the fact that he is divinely chosen.

It is like a little boy answered when someone said to him after he had been saved, ''Son, did you find Jesus?'' The little boy very sincerely said, ''I didn't know Jesus was lost. Jesus found me.''

Friend, that is what happened to you who are saved. To have Christ in your life. means you have been divinely chosen. I am sure your mind could reminisce, as mine does, of how the Lord, in the midst of religion, in the midst of Bible ignorance, in infinite mercy, laid His hand on you and saved you. He selected this country boy, chose me, and I have been His ever since.

A lot of folks say some are predestined to go to Heaven. It is not taught in the Bible that a person is predestined to go to Heaven. It is taught in the Bible that you are predestined to be like Christ.

There is no such thing as God's choosing some and God's saying to others, ''You cannot be saved.'' If any man be lost, he is lost because he chooses to be. If you are saved, God has predestined you to be like His Son. If you are a Christian, God will make you like Him and He will work in your life to that end. When the Lord comes, we will then find the consummation of our salvation. And even these bodies shall be redeemed and we shall be like Him. ''Beloved, now are we the sons of God, and it doth not yet appear what we shall be: but we know that, when he shall appear, we shall be like him; for we shall see him as he is'' (I John 3:2). Romans 8:29 says, ''For whom he did foreknow, he also did predestinate to be conformed to the image of his Son. . . .'' God is in the process of making us Christlike. That is His whole purpose. We are predestined to be conformed to the image of His Son.

One time a new convert was asked, ''Do you know the doctrine of election and predestination?''

He answered, "Sure."

People were surprised, "Then explain it to us."

He gave this explanation: "There were three votes. The Devil voted against me and Jesus voted for me. I untied the vote by voting for myself to be a Christian."

Friend, that is a decision that every man and woman must make in life or be lost. He has chosen you. Have you chosen Him?

Nathanael was divinely chosen. I like that. I will never forget when it dawned on me shortly after I was saved that my getting saved in that little country church as a nineteen-year-old boy in the summer of 1935 did not take God by surprise. The Lord knew I was going to get saved in that meeting. The Lord laid His hand on me. God chose me. That makes me know God has a purpose for my life. He puts all the power of the Trinity and all the resources of Heaven behind that life to make it Christlike and fruitful. That is true also of your life.

II. NATHANAEL WAS WON BY ANOTHER

You may think the preachers in this place seem to talk so much about the fact that one person is won by another. Take your Bible and study about the disciples, then you will find that God used somebody to win them. There is no conflict between the fact that Nathanael was divinely chosen but humanly won. That is the way everybody is won. God uses people.

Nathanael was won by the testimony of Philip who said, "We have found him." Philip did not say anything profound. He did not know much about the plan of salvation; he did not know much about theology—but he knew that Christ was the Son of God, so he said, "Nathanael, we have found Him."

God took that simple testimony and revolutionized the life of another. God wants us to be able to say to any man, woman, boy or girl, "We have found Him. We know Christ as our personal Saviour."

Philip was a smart soul winner. When Nathanael said, "Can any good thing come out of Nazareth?" Philip did not say, "Let me explain to you the doctrine of the virgin birth, or the deity of Jesus, or the doctrine of salvation by grace." He just said, "Come and see."

I am thrilled when I think of the maniac of Gadara. When he got saved, he said to Jesus, "I want to follow You." Jesus suffered him not but said, "Go home to thy friends and tell them what great things the Lord hath done for thee."

A man in this church (now with the Lord) was very successful in reaching people for Jesus. He did not know much. He would just reach out and get hold of people and bring them to the Lord. It amazed me. I have seen him go to people, say three or four words and those people would start forward. He brought literally dozens down this aisle.

One day I went to where he was in a small business. He worked alone. I went to his office. I never saw such a man in my life. He was not handsome, he didn't have the greatest personality in the world, but he would just reach out and lay hold of somebody for Jesus, just like picking apples off a tree. I wanted to find out about that fellow. There was something about him that was miraculous. So I went to his office to see him. I said, "Friend, what in the world is it about you? You draw people to Christ like a person drawing in fish." I, a preacher, had to humble myself. I said, "What do you say to them?"

He answered me like this: "Tom, years ago when I lived in Detroit, I was the worst drunk in the world. Nobody had any hope for me. I literally drank my family down the drain. But one day a person came to me and said, 'You know, the Lord can save you. I too was a drunk and an alcoholic, and the Lord saved me. The Lord can change your whole life.' Brother Tom, the Lord reached down in the gutter, got hold of me and saved me. Since then

I have just been telling people what Jesus did for me.''

I said, ''I have seen you go to total strangers, folks you had never laid eyes on, reach out to them and here they came. What do you say to them?''

He replied, ''Just what I told you. I tell them the Lord has done great things for me. I tell them I was an alcoholic and He saved me. I tell them that He can save them, no matter how deep in sin they may be. That is all I know. That is all God told us to tell people.''

''Come and see,'' Philip said and Nathanael was won. There was no conflict between the divine choosing and human effort. Some think there is. You hear some in this country talk about Calvinism. There are those who say, ''If the Lord wants to do something, He will do it. He does not need human effort.'' That is not Bible. God always uses men. If you doubt that, you think of how the Lord Jesus, who made worlds, when He was ready to come to earth and die to save people, chose the body of a little Jewish maiden and came by a mother's womb. He used a human body.

Jesus, at the pool of Bethesda, said to a man, ''Wilt thou be made whole?'' The man with an infirmity answered, ''Sir, I have no man, when the water is troubled, to put me into the pool.''

Lost souls need someone to tell them about Jesus Christ. ''Now then we are ambassadors for Christ, as though God did beseech you by us: we pray you in Christ's stead, be ye reconciled to God'' (II Cor. 5:20). Paul is saying, ''I am standing in Jesus' shoes. In Christ's stead, I am reaching out a hand for Jesus and beseeching that you be saved.''

See Jesus on the cross, His hands nailed where mine ought to be, His feet nailed where mine ought to be, His side riven with a spear where mine should have been, His head crowned with thorns that should have rested on my head. See Him in my place on the cross. God wants to see you today in His place in the world. Jesus has no hands but ours. He has no feet, no lips, no eyes but ours. He says today, ''You stand in My stead and beseech people to be saved.'' That is what it is all about. This is what the Devil freezes people up about more than anything else. He does not want them to believe God wants to use them.

I have seen many people saved in the 38 years God has allowed me the tremendous privilege of preaching the Gospel. I was thinking of a call to my home about 4:30 a.m. from a mother whom I later met. She said, ''My son, an officer in the Marines, has been home. He is leaving today and his whole life is troubled. Can you see him? He must leave early.'' I said, ''I can meet him in about 15 minutes in my office.'' About 4:45 that morning a white-haired mother and her grown son, a handsome man, came to my office. He walked in as straight as a two-by-four. During the conversation he said, ''Yes, I got what I wanted in the service. I am an officer and fixed for life as far as material things are concerned. But I do not know God and I want to be saved.''

At 5:00 a.m., almost to the minute, in my office a big Marine and his white-haired mother got down on their knees and that Marine got saved. God spoke to his heart, saying, ''Son, without Christ you are lost.'' God said to a Christian, ''You get out of bed, get over there and get that man saved.'' No conflict between the two: the work of God and human effort.

Nathanael was chosen of the Lord and was humanly won.

III. HE WAS KNOWN BY THE LORD

Nathanael was known by the Lord. There is some interesting dialogue here between Jesus and Nathanael. ''Jesus saw Nathanael coming to him, and saith of him, Behold an Israelite indeed, in whom is no guile!'' (John 1:47). I will talk about that later. When Jesus said there was no guile found in this man, He never meant he was not sinful, never meant he did not need to be saved.

"Nathanael saith unto him, Whence knowest thou me? Jesus answered and said unto him, Before that Philip called thee, when thou wast under the fig tree, I saw thee" (vs. 48). "Whence knowest thou me?" asked Nathanael of the Lord of Heaven. He said, "Before Philip ever spoke to you sitting under that fig tree, I saw thee." Around the other side of the mountain, Jesus saw through the rocks and dirt, granite and stone and into the heart of a man, because He knows everything and everybody.

Nathanael was known of the Lord. The Bible says, "The eyes of the Lord are in every place, beholding the evil and the good" (Prov. 15:3). We read in Jeremiah 16:17, "For mine eyes are upon all their ways: they are not hid from my face, neither is their iniquity hid from mine eyes." And Hebrews 4:13 says, "Neither is there any creature that is not manifest in his sight: but all things are naked and opened unto the eyes of him with whom we have to do."

The Lord knew Nathanael. He saw him before Nathanael ever saw Jesus. The Lord knew everything about him. The hairs of his head were numbered by the Lord. He knew his age, his name, his background, his future. He was completely diagnosed, known and x-rayed by the Lord.

God knows you today. It is like the man who for 29 years had been able to say to himself, *I committed the perfect crime.* He had committed murder 29 years before and had not been caught.

One day two police officers after 29 years, knocked on his door and said, "Are you So-and-so?"

"Yes."

"We have come to arrest you."

He said, "For 29 years I have lived with this. I am glad now that you have come." He very meekly walked away with them.

Listen, the Lord knows whether or not you are saved. You can fool me; that would not be hard to do. And you may fool others: but the Lord knows whether or not you are saved. The Lord knows if your heart is burdened. He never misses a fallen tear, nor ever fails to hear a tired sigh. Knowing all about you, He still loves you and reaches out to you. Will you come to Him?

IV. NATHANAEL WAS A LOST, DEPRAVED SINNER

When Jesus saw Nathanael coming to Him, Jesus made a statement that I do not know He ever made about any other individual: "Behold an Israelite indeed, in whom is no guile!" The word "guile" means "deceit" or "hypocrisy." Jesus was not saying that Nathanael was sinless and perfect. He merely said he was sincere about what he believed. The Lord showed him that he was wrong about what he believed.

People can be sincere—and be sincerely wrong. They can think they are right when they are not. This was true of Nathanael. Jesus said, "Here is a Jew indeed, in whom there is no deceit." He was saying that Nathanael was sincere about what he believed, but he was sincerely wrong.

Nathanael was a lost sinner, a depraved human being without God and without hope.

This leads me to the doctrine, so clearly taught in the Bible, of the total depravity of human nature. You may say, "What is so important about the doctrine of depravity? How corrupt, how undone, how lost, how godless man is—what is so important about that?" It is so important because it is a basic teaching of the Bible. If this is not true, the new birth is not needed. If this is not true, there is no explanation to why Jesus would go to the cross. If man is not depraved, the whole plan of redemption is without meaning. But the Bible plainly teaches the depravity of man.

Read both Old Testament and New Testament and see how God pulls the veneer off all humanity. God opens up, as it were, the human heart and shows us the inside of man and what he is like without Christ. The total depravity of human nature is taught in the Word of God.

Isaiah mentioned it in the great mountain peak of prophetical teaching of atonement and redemption, in Isaiah 53:6: "All we like sheep have gone astray; we have turned every one to his own way; and the Lord hath laid on him the iniquity of us all."

A sheep is the most dumb animal in some ways, in the animal kingdom. Take a dog and go hunting with him, lose him, go back home the ten miles and the next morning he will be waiting on the porch for you to feed him. Dogs know their way around. Take an old cat, put it in a sack, tie the sack up, put the sack in the trunk of the car and haul Mr. Cat miles away. Then turn him loose and a lot of times Mr. Cat will be home before you get there.

On the other hand, a sheep is a geographical moron. Take him around behind the barn and he will get lost. He cannot get back to the front without help. He will cry and complain, but he does not know where he is, and he does not know how to get back where he should be.

Isaiah said, "All we like sheep have gone astray; we have turned every one to his own way . . . ." The depravity of human nature is inherited from birth. This is hereditary. The Bible plainly teaches we are born in sin and conceived in iniquity. In Jeremiah 17:9 we read, "The heart is deceitful above all things, and desperately wicked: who can know it?" The heart is the most deceitful thing in all the world. Man is totally depraved.

Romans 4 shows how God justifies believers. Romans 3 paints a darker background. The Lord is about to lay some beautiful diamond of truth out here, so He spreads a piece of black velvet, on which to put that beautiful gem. Romans 3 shows God literally pulling the veneer off a human being so you can look inside, "As it is written, There is none righteous, no, not one" (vs. 10).

Somebody says, "Well, I know someone who is righteous." God says, "There is none righteous." Dear friend, until you are born the second time, you are depraved and eternally lost, according to Romans 3:12: "They are all gone out of the way, they are together become unprofitable; there is none that doeth good, no, not one."

I have heard people say, "I know sinners who do good. They help people when their houses burn down. They take people baskets at Christmas time. They help their neighbors." But the Bible says they are all gone out of the way, they are unprofitable, there is none that doeth good.

Now look at Romans 3:19, "Now we know that what things soever the law saith, it saith to them who are under the law: that every mouth may be stopped, and all the world may become guilty before God." God said, "I have said these things that every mouth may be stopped. I don't want anybody trying to justify himself by saying, 'I am good enough for Heaven and I don't need to be cleansed in the blood.' Let every mouth be stopped and the whole world become guilty."

As Dr. Henry Joe Hankins used to say, "You have to preach men lost before you can preach men saved." That is what the Bible says, too. The Lord was not saying that Nathanael was not a sinner, because Romans 3:23 says, "...all have sinned, and come short of the glory of God."

Take a man like Nicodemus. He would be hard to win. But go in the slums of our city and find some fellow in the dope business or one who drinks—a parasite on human society—and say to that person, "You are lost. You are depraved." He would more often than not say, "You are right. I know I am lost, depraved."

Here is Nicodemus dressed in all of his religious finery; he prays three times a day, fasts twice a week and tithes his income. But Jesus said, "Ye must be born again, Nicodemus, because you are depraved." Nicodemus was just as depraved as the man in the gutter.

These modernists say everybody has a little good in them and all you have to do is just fan a little bit and it will spring up. I have for many years seen modernists do a lot of that fanning but they do not get people born again. People do not get saved until they know they are lost and without God.

I read a little story the other day. It said that some animal lovers had decided that lions and tigers would not be all that bad if they were raised right. So they took some little lion cubs, fed them warm milk and tried to love them to death after being told a lion, if it is fed right and loved right, will never hurt anybody.

One of those little cubs got to be a big lion. One day one of these people was watching him. There was a donkey nearby. That eleven-month-old lion ran, jumped on the back of that donkey and sunk his claws into him. Then he reached out with one of his paws and pulled his head. With his teeth, he gouged into his jugular vein, and down went Mr. Donkey, lion and all, rolling and blood flying everywhere. Do you know why? There is a lion's nature in that animal which cannot be cultivated out of him.

There is a fallen nature in men and women. So the only hope for them is an experience called the new birth.

Nathanael was a lost, depraved sinner whom the Lord saved.

V. NATHANAEL HAD AN EXCUSE
NOT TO BE SAVED

Nathanael had an excuse not to be saved. I did not say he had a reason. No one has a reason, but he had an excuse. When Philip said, "Nathanael, we have found him of whom the Bible speaks," Nathanael had an excuse. He says, "Can there any good thing come out of Nazareth?" (John 1:46). He had heard of that wicked city. It is a most unfriendly city even today. A group of us were there some years ago. We were getting a drink at what is called Mary's Well and people began to throw things at us.

Thinking of that wicked city, he said, "You mean someone from Nazareth is good, holy, righteous and divine? Could that One be my Saviour? I don't believe that." Nathanael was skeptical about the whole thing. He thought he had an excuse not to be a Christian. But he didn't. No one has an excuse to reject Jesus Christ as the Son of God.

I guess I have heard them all. I have heard people say, "Well, now, I am waiting until another time." What that really means is they are rejecting Jesus Christ. Second Corinthians 6:2, "...behold, now is the accepted time; behold, now is the day of salvation." God said "now." Man says "not now."

A man was sitting on the corner of this platform some years ago who had broken one of his legs. He had a cast on it up to his knee. Somebody had brought him to church. They said to me, "Preacher, we want you to talk to this gentleman. He needs to be saved."

I began talking to him. He said, "I want to be saved sometime, but not now."

I said, "You are saying not now but the Bible says now." I quoted Isaiah 1:18, "Come now, and let us reason together, saith the Lord: though your sins be as scarlet, they shall be as white as snow; though they be red like crimson, they shall be as wool."

He said, "No, not now." Finally he looked at me and said, "I will tell you what I will do, Preacher. I will be saved tonight."

I said to him, "If you are, you will be the first one who ever turned down the Lord and said not now who ever kept his word about when he would be saved."

He said, "I am going to be that one. I promise you I will be saved tonight."

I said, "The Bible says now. God says now."

He said, "No, not now but I will be here tonight."

He left with the friend who had brought him. Two or three of our people heard him. "Do you think he will come?" they asked.

I said, "He won't be here."

They said, "Preacher, have faith!"

I said, "I am not going to have faith in humanity and a lost, depraved person."

They said, "Preacher, you may be wrong. He may come."

I said, "No, he won't come."

They looked at me as if they were thinking, *Well, that smart aleck, he doesn't know everything. He doesn't know whether he is coming or not.*

Do you know why I knew he was not coming? They never do. God says, "Now!" When a man says, "Not now," he is saying, "I don't want God."

Nathanael thought he had an excuse. I have had people say to me, "Now, Preacher, you talk about that being saved all you want to, but I am as good as some of your church members." I always say, "That is exactly right. Most anybody is as good as some of our church members." When a fellow says, "I am as good as some of your church members," he is not being complimentary. Some may be as crooked as a corkscrew and when they die, you will have to screw them into the ground.

What goodness looks like in the eyes of God is recorded in Isaiah 64:6, "But we are all as an unclean thing, and all our righteousnesses are as filthy rags." God did not say all of our unrighteousnesses are as filthy rags. He said if we are not saved, all we try to do that is good is like a filthy rag in the eyes of a holy God.

How foolish for a man to say, "I can do good while my foot is in the blood of Jesus Christ. While I am spitting in the face of the Son of God, I will do good things." When a man says,

"I am as good as some church member," that excuse will not stand the test of the judgment day.

I have had them say to me, "Preacher, there are too many hypocrites in the church." If there is one, that is too many. But if a fellow says he is not a Christian because there are hypocrites in the church, he is the biggest hypocrite of them all. If you are hiding behind that, then you are smaller than the hypocrite. Let me illustrate!

You cannot hide a book behind a pencil. Do you know why? That book is bigger than the pencil. You never thought of that, did you? If I am getting over your head, I will slow down. But I can hide a pencil behind a book. Do you know why? That book is bigger than that pencil. A man who is trying to hide behind a hypocrite is smaller than the hypocrite. What a flimsy excuse to turn down the Son of God!

There are hypocrite lawyers, hypocrite doctors, and hypocrite grocerymen. When I want a doctor, I will get me a good one. When I want a lawyer, I will get a good one. There are shysters in every profession. People know that. But when it comes to being saved, they say, "There are too many hypocrites in the church."

Then I have had them say, "Yes, Preacher, this is all so, but you know, I don't feel anything." In the first place, you would not know it if you felt it. Salvation is not by feeling, it is by faith. When a fellow says, "I know I ought to be saved but I just don't feel like it," I think of Ephesians 2:1, "And you hath he quickened, who were dead in trespasses and sins...."

The Bible says plainly that one who is not saved is dead, not physically but spiritually. Can you imagine a dead man saying, "I don't feel anything!" If he did, we would soon clear a path to exit!

Here is a book that weighs about eight ounces. Pretend it is a person. Now you lie down there. You are dead. I put something on your chest. Do you feel that? No. Dead people feel nothing. You say, "It is not heavy enough." Get something that weighs 100 pounds and put it on this dead person's chest. "Do you feel anything?" No. You say, "But that is not heavy enough." Okay, put this piano on this dead man, then ask him, "Do you feel anything?" No, not a thing. Why? Because he is dead! You are not supposed to feel anything when you are dead.

You have to know that apart from Christ, you are lost. And Christ came to save that which is lost, those dead in their sins.

Some fellow says, "Well, I will take my chances." How ridiculous! "For what shall it profit a man, if he shall gain the whole world, and lose his own soul?" (Mark 8:36). You do not have one chance in twenty billion. No chance! For a man, woman, boy or girl who is not saved, there is no chance. There is no excuse for not being saved.

I have had them say to me, "I am waiting for somebody else." I have had women literally weep and say, "Preacher, I would like to be saved, but I am waiting for my husband to be saved." Or, I have had men say, "I am waiting for my wife." Or, "I am waiting for a friend." Proverbs 27:1 says, "Boast not thyself of to morrow; for thou knowest not what a day may bring forth."

Somebody else says, "Well, I will tell you what my excuse is: I don't believe the Bible."

The Bible is a sword. A fellow says, "I don't believe that is a sword." Do you know one way to prove it to him? Just take the point of it and stick it in his body! "Now do you believe it?" "Whoo, do I believe it!" That is what to do with the Bible. When a fellow says, "I don't believe the Bible," stick him with it. Push it in him. Make a believer out of him.

Years ago a student at Moody Bible Institute was talking to a man on the street who had said, "I don't believe that is the Word of God."

The student said, "It is appointed unto man once to die, but after that the judgment."

The other one said, "I told you I don't believe that."

The student said, "But it is appointed unto man once to die, but after that the judgment."

The fellow said, "I told you I don't believe that!"

The student repeated, "But it is appointed unto man once to die, but after that the judgment."

The fellow, mellow now, hung his head and said, "If after death there comes judgment, then tell me how to be saved."

If you do not believe the Bible, wait until judgment day. John 3:18 says, "He that believeth on him is not condemned: but he that believeth not is condemned already, because he hath not believed in the name of the only begotten Son of God." At the judgment day, if you are lost, what will your excuse be? In the judgment day, when God takes His books and begins to read, "And whosoever was not found written in the book of life was cast into the lake of fire," what are you going to tell Him then? (Rev. 20:15). God will say to you, "Is your name in here?" "No." You could never fabricate an excuse to stand the test of the hot fire of God's judgment day, when He reads from the Book, "And whosoever was not found written in the book of life was cast into the lake of fire."

There is absolutely no excuse for not being a Christian.

VI. NATHANAEL BELIEVED IN THE DEITY OF CHRIST

Nathanael believed in the deity of Christ. This brings before us the tremendous, all-essential doctrine of the deity of our Lord and Saviour, Jesus Christ.

When Jesus said to Nathanael, "I saw you sitting under the fig tree. I was around on the other side of the mountain, but I saw you just the same. Through rock, stone, clay and dirt, I saw you," do you know what Nathanael said? "Thou art the Son of God. You are the Son of God. You are the One to be the King of Israel. You are the Son of God." Then he was saved immediately.

I want to say to you without reservation, no one can be saved who does not believe Jesus Christ is the Son of God. No Mohammedan can be saved who says He is an equal to Abraham but is not God. No one who says, "I know He is a good teacher and the personification of love, kindness, mercy, but I am not sure who He is," can be saved until you know He is the Son of God.

First Timothy 2:5 says, "For there is one God, and one mediator between God and men, the man Christ Jesus." In Matthew 16:13-16 we read,

"When Jesus came into the coasts of Caesarea Philippi, he asked his disciples, saying, Whom do men say that I the Son of man am? And they said, Some say that thou art John the Baptist: some, Elias; and others, Jeremias, or one of the prophets. He saith unto them, But whom say ye that I am? And Simon Peter answered and said, Thou art the Christ, the Son of the living God."

Jesus said, "Blessed art thou, Simon Barjona: for flesh and blood hath not revealed it unto thee, but my Father which is in heaven" (vs. 17).

You cannot be saved without believing Jesus is the Son of God. A modernist who says that Jesus is not the Son of God is a lost infidel and he is going to Hell.

Nels Ferre said that Jesus could have easily been the product of a blond German soldier and a Jewish woman. Unless he changed his belief, he went to Hell. To doubt His deity is to damn one's soul.

Nathanael said, "You are the Son of God. You are Deity."

When Jesus was baptized and He was about to be taken into the wilderness, He had not eaten for 40 days and nights. Satan said, "If thou be the Son of God, command that these stones be made bread" (Matt. 4:3).

I thank God there is no "if" in our doctrine, our belief about the deity of Jesus Christ. I know He is God's Son. I have many reasons to know: I know it for one reason above all others. In 1935 He stepped across the threshold of my trembling heart and brought with Him all the glories of Heaven. He spoke peace, cleanness and forgiveness to my soul. He did for me, in that glorious moment, what only God can do. So, with Nathanael, ten million angels and others, I declare, "Thou art the Son of God!"

They kept saying to Jesus, "Show us a sign. Prove Your deity."

Jesus answered them in Matthew 12:38-40:

"An evil and adulterous generation seeketh after a sign; and there shall no sign be given to it, but the sign of the prophet Jonas: For as Jonas was three days and three nights in the whale's belly; so shall the Son of man be three days and three nights in the heart of the earth."

After three days and three nights in the sleeping clay, the Spirit of God breathed and the stone rolled away. An earthquake came and Jesus stepped out and said, "I am alive for evermore."

"Nathanael answered and saith unto him, Rabbi, thou art the Son of God...."

VII. NATHANAEL WAS A SPIRIT-FILLED BELIEVER

Nathanael was a powerful Christian. He was filled with the Holy Spirit of God. There is no question about it.

Acts 1:13, 14 says:

"And when they were come in, they went up into an upper room, where abode both Peter, and James, and John, and Andrew, Philip, and Thomas, Bartholomew [Nathanael], *and Matthew, James the son of Alphaeus, and Simon Zelotes, and Judas the brother*

of James. These all continued with one accord in prayer...."

Nathanael was in that Upper Room before Pentecost. He was praying because Jesus had said just going away, "Tarry ye in Jerusalem till you be endued with power from on high." "That is what I want," said Nathanael. Jesus said in Acts 1:8, "But ye shall receive power, after that the Holy Ghost is come upon you: and ye shall be witnesses unto me both in Jerusalem, and in all Judaea, and in Samaria, and unto the uttermost part of the earth."

Waiting in that Upper Room was Nathanael, who that day under a fig tree looked at Jesus and heard Him speak. He believed in Him as the Son of God and was saved. When the day of Pentecost was fully come, Nathanael was baptized in and filled with the Holy Ghost.

Nathanael is mentioned 25 times in the book of Acts. Twenty-five times in the book of Acts it speaks of the apostles, of their power, their preaching, their soul winning, their great lives, and their miracles. Nathanael was one of them. Nathanael had the power of God on his life. Do you?

Some time ago I was preaching in Houston, Texas to a full house, including many preachers and college students. I was talking about, "Not by might, nor by power, but by my spirit, saith the Lord of hosts" (Zech. 4:6). At the close of the service people began to come. It looked as if the windows of Heaven opened. The front of the church was filled. People were looking for a place to get right with God.

One young man came, gripped my hand and said, "You know my father. I want you to pray with me." He almost pulled me down. We went down to the altar together. He said to me, sobbing, "God called me to preach three years ago. I went to school, then dropped out; went again and dropped out. The reason I have given up the call to the ministry is because I have never known the power of God. I know I am saved, but I don't have the power of God in my life.''

We prayed and waited before God. The Lord was doing wonderful things in the lives of others. Then this young man said, ''I would like to say a word.'' The pastor said, ''Come on, young man.'' He came up to the platform and said, ''I want to say this to you publicly. You have seen me fail, you have known how weak I am. But I believe tonight God got hold of my life.''

The power of God—Nathanael had it. Do you have the power of God? Do you know that God's power works through you like an electrical current? Do you know the reality of God's power in your life?

Nathanael knew that. What the Lord did in the life of this skeptic, He can do in any life that is laid at His feet and surrendered to His will.

''Nathanael answered and saith unto him, Rabbi, thou art the Son of God....''— John 1:49.

Chapter VIII

Thomas, the Doubter

READ: Mark 3:6-21.

"And Thomas answered unto him, My Lord and my God." — John 20:28.

One of the twelve times that Thomas is mentioned in the New Testament is found here in this passage. Look at Mark 3:18: "And Andrew, and Philip, and Bartholomew, and Matthew, and Thomas, and James the son of Alphaeus, and Thaddaeus, and Simon the Canaanite."

I doubt if in all the history of the human race there have ever been living simultaneously twelve more significant men than the twelve disciples whom Jesus chose. You find them listed four times in the New Testament, in Matthew, Mark and Luke; then again in the book of Acts. Simon Peter is always named first, though I do not know why. Judas Iscariot is always named last and I think I do know why. It is because he is one who made himself infamous by his unbelief, infidelity and disloyalty as he betrayed the Lord and sold Him for thirty pieces of silver.

These are significant men. With them Jesus deposited His truth while He was upon the earth for three and a half years. To them He entrusted the great task of preaching the Gospel to the then known world. To a number of them He entrusted the tremendous responsibility of writing books which we have, inspired of God, in the Holy Bible. I do not believe there has ever been a more influential group of men than these. If you doubt that, you need but to drive down the streets of your city. You will find churches named after Peter and Paul and James and John and most of these other disciples, these twelve very significant men.

I want to talk to you tonight about one of them. I suppose you could say I was named after him. He is the first man in the Bible as far as we know whose name was Thomas. What does the Bible say about Thomas? He is mentioned four times in a complete list of the disciples. All we know of his characteristics we find in one book, the Gospel of John where he is found in eight different verses of Scripture. In the Gospel of John we have a characteristic picture of Thomas.

Tradition tells us that Thomas died preaching the Word of God. Some say that he preached as far away as Babylon. Finally, one day while he was preaching someone thrust a lance through his body and he died a martyr for Christ.

You say, "Preacher, why study about a man?" Because much of the truth in the Bible God clothed around a human personality. If you doubt that, you only have to think of Noah. The first time grace is mentioned in the Bible it is mentioned in connection with Noah. "But Noah found grace in the eyes of the Lord" (Gen. 6:8).

God clothes much of the teaching of faith and trust around a man named Abraham; then in the fourth chapter of Romans we read, "Abraham believed God, and it was counted unto him for righteousness" (vs. 3). I am saying that God clothes the truth of His Word around human personalities.

Of whom could you learn more about stedfastness than from a Daniel? Of whom could you learn more about human failure in the life of a Christian than from David? Of whom could you learn more about the Gospel of God's grace and the imputed righteousness of the Son of God than by studying the life of a converted rabbi, Paul the apostle? Of whom could you learn more about love than from John whose life the Lord clothed with His great doctrine and teaching of love?

The Bible teaches that what I am saying is so. God takes great truths from the Bible and clothes them around human personalities. Titus 2:10, "Not purloining, but shewing all good fidelity; that they may adorn the doctrine of God our Saviour in all things." Every lady here knows what cosmetics are. But do you know what the word "cosmetics" means? That word is actually found in the Bible, in this verse, "Not purloining, but shewing all good fidelity; that they may adorn...." The Greek word *kosmeo* from which we get our word "cosmetics" is used here. "...that they may adorn...." or dress up, or make look better, "...the doctrine of God our Saviour in all things." In fact, God teaches us that every Christian's life is to exemplify the doctrinal teaching of the Word of God. That is what Paul meant when he said, "Ye are our epistle written in our hearts, known and read of all men" (II Cor. 3:2).

Thomas shows that our testimony follows us long after we are gone. Nineteen hundred long, dusty years are between us and the time he lived. How many times have I heard people say, "Thomas was a doubter"; or they call him "Thomas, the doubter." In fact, I have friends affectionately call me "Doubting Thomas." This man's testimony has lingered in connection with his name for nineteen hundred years. I would like you to see five sides to this man, Thomas.

I. HE WAS NOT WHERE HE SHOULD HAVE BEEN

First, he was not where he should be all of the time. One of the most outstanding pictures of Thomas in the Bible is found when Jesus arose from the dead. Jesus rose from the dead on Sunday. The Bible tells us of that evening He appeared in the Upper Room where the disciples were gathered together for fear of the Jews. The Scripture says something very significantly: "But Thomas...was not with them...." (John 20:24). The very first Sunday night church service, Thomas missed! He was not where he should have been! That has been true of a lot of Christians. Thomas missed the very first Sunday evening church service ever held in the Christian church this side of the death, burial and resurrection of Jesus Christ.

The Bible has something to say about our being where the Lord's people are. See from the Bible the tremendous importance God puts on a Christian being where there is Christian fellowship. Hebrews 10:25 says, "Not forsaking the assembling of ourselves together, as the manner of some is; but exhorting one another: and so much the more, as ye see the day approaching." That tremendous verse says, 'Don't forsake assembling of yourselves together.' Nineteen hundred years ago people were guilty of not going to church and not having Christian fellowship and being where they should be. The Bible said nineteen hundred years ago, 'Don't forsake the assembling of yourselves together, as the manner of some is; but exhort one another and so much the more as ye see the day approaching.' The Lord says that a Christian should be in the Christian family and the Christian fellowship because the Lord is coming! When He comes, that is the place to be found. See an illustration of what I am talking about.

On that first Sunday all of us have read where two men left the city of Jerusalem and were walking out to Emmaus—a long walk. I have taken that journey in a car along the road from Jerusalem to the little community of Emmaus. While walking along, One suddenly appears in step with them, One they do not recognize. They talk with Him; they say to Him very sadly, "Have you heard what happened in Jerusalem? Jesus was crucified three days ago, the One we had hoped would be the Messiah, but they crucified

Him and buried Him in a tomb.'' They were on their way out to Emmaus. As they walk along, finally Jesus reveals Himself unto them.

Listen to Luke 24:13: "And, behold, two of them went that same day to a village called Emmaus, which was from Jerusalem about threescore furlongs.'' They should have been in Jerusalem, back where the Lord had told them He would meet with them! But here they are on their way to Emmaus. When Jesus appeared to them, "their eyes were holden that they should not know him'' (vs. 16). They did not even recognize Him. When He revealed Himself, notice what they did. "And they rose up the same hour, and returned to Jerusalem, and found the eleven gathered together, and them that were with them'' (vs. 33). These men said, "We'd better get where Christians are!'' That is true of every Christian. Thomas was guilty of not being where he should have been.

You should ask yourself, "Where should I be?'' A Christian should be in the house of the Lord. No board member has any right to miss the scheduled services of his church. No Sunday school teacher is worthy of the name who would deliberately absent herself or himself from fellowship with the saints of God. The Bible teaches that going where the Lord's people are is one of the signs of a truly born-again Christian. A lot of these people who come every once in awhile and hold down eighteen inches of padded seat are not going to be there when the roll is called up yonder. One of the characteristics of a saved person is that he desires and wants and recognizes his need of fellowship with other Christians. "I was glad when they said unto me, Let us go into the house of the Lord'' (Ps. 122:1). Thomas was not where he should have been.

A preacher was called to be a missionary. He got the chance to pastor a church. He was an oratorical and gifted speaker. He preached to a full church as a result of his gift and good preaching.

But nobody got saved. No blessings came. No people were baptized. When nobody was being led to the Lord and to the church, he said, "I must be in the wrong place." God had called him to the mission field.

He went on to another church, hoping to find fruitfulness in his service. The same thing happened there. Many people came to hear him, but nothing happened. No lives were changed, no people were converted. Finally, with a broken heart, he said, "There is only one place I will ever find happiness and that is on the mission field where God called me!"

I am saying, there are appointed places where God wants a Christian to be and peace, happiness and fruitfulness will never be found anywhere else in the world.

Thomas was guilty of not being where he should be.

II. HE WAS GUILTY OF THE SIN OF DOUBTING

Thomas was guilty of the sin that everybody in this room has committed, including this preacher. Thomas' besetting sin was that he doubted. His besetting sin was that he could not believe without seeing. He could not believe without touching. He could not believe without feeling. He could not believe just because God said so. So Thomas was guilty of the sin of doubt.

It is a strange thing. He was not in church when the disciples met and the Lord appeared to them. The disciples said to Thomas, "We have seen the Lord." Thomas threw a bucket of cold water on the whole meeting. (That is typical of folks who do not go to church, typical of what folks do who are not where they should be. They want to dampen the spirits of those who do get happy and who do have some thrills in serving the Lord.) Thomas said, "Except I shall see in his hands the print of the nails, and put my finger into the print of the nails, and thrust my hand into his side, I will not believe" (John 20:25). He said, "If I can't feel

I'm not going to believe because of what I've heard." The Bible says, "So then faith cometh by hearing, and hearing by the word of God" (Rom. 10:17). Thomas said, "I won't believe unless I see, unless I feel; I'll not believe just by hearing."

Thomas has come to us through these nineteen centuries as a man guilty of doubt: "Unless I can feel the nail wounds...." That is a significant thing about the Bible. When a person was crucified, they could put nails in his hands or not put nails in his hands. Many were crucified by people taking leather thongs and binding their arms to the cross beam and their feet to the cross, with no nails being used.

In the book of Psalms, it is prophesied, "...they pierced my hands and my feet" (22:16). When Thomas said, "I will not believe unless I see the prints of the nails in his hands," the Old Testament foretold that Jesus would be nailed to the cross, not bound to it.

Not a person here has not had to fight and to pray against the sin of doubt in your life! Why do people doubt? I think there are three basic reasons.

They doubt, in the first place, because they have not hid the Word of God in their heart. A Christian who does not read the Bible, a Christian who does not have the promises, a Christian who does not hide it in his heart and in his inner life, is bound to doubt.

Thomas said, "I will not believe unless I can see." He was taking the position opposite from that of hearing the testimony and accepting the truth. No Christian is going to be without doubt unless he has the Bible hidden in his heart. The psalmist said, "Thy word have I hid in mine heart, that I might not sin against thee" (119:11).

I took one piece of the Word of God and for three and a half years I lived with it every day. It was Philippians 4:19, "But my God shall supply all your need according to his riches in glory by Christ Jesus.'' From 1939 and for three and a half years later, I depended on it.

I do not know how many thousands of miles I have flown in a plane; twenty-one times to the Middle East and back, all over Europe and many places. I went many places in small planes for twenty-seven years. I always had one promise, one part of the Word of God, that took the fear out of my heart.

I was walking out of the hotel lobby in 1956 to get on a plane, prop planes then. It took thirteen hours to fly from New York City to a little island, a little speck out in the Atlantic Ocean called St. Helena in the Azores. As I was walking out of the lobby there were great big block letter headlines on the newspaper, "PLANE DOWN IN THE ATLANTIC." Don't think that won't cause you to pray! I did not even buy that paper. I didn't want any details. I wanted a verse from the Word of God. I thought of one—"The eternal God is thy refuge, and underneath are the everlasting arms" (Deut. 33:27). Every time since then when I have gotten on a plane I have always said it: "The eternal God is thy refuge, and underneath are the everlasting arms." A Christian will doubt when he does not saturate his heart and mind with the Word of God.

Believing the promises of God means believing them because God said it. We do not need sight, nor sound, nor feeling. We can believe it is God who is speaking, and God cannot lie. Jesus said to Thomas, "Thomas, because thou hast seen me, thou hast believed: blessed are they that have not seen, and yet have believed" (John 20:29).

First John 5:13 tells me that if I believe, I have eternal life. I claim that. I rest upon that. This Bible tells me if I believe, I have eternal life. I know I am saved! People ask, "Preacher, how do you know you are saved?" "Because the Bible says so," I answer. Some folks say in answer to that question, "Because I feel like

I am." I do not always feel like I am saved. I really do not feel too much that way tonight. I have had a "bug" and I have been chewing aspirins all day.

I know I am saved because this blessed Book of God tells me that I am a Christian and that Christ is in my life and Heaven is my home and the Holy Spirit dwells in me! I know it because God said it! When a person doubts, it is because he has not hidden the Word of God in his heart. "These things have I written unto you that believe on the name of the Son of God; that ye may know that ye have eternal life. . ." (I John 5:13).

About prayer. You will never be able to pray and believe until you pray in connection with the Bible! Take a promise from the Word of God. Take that promise and hold it up to God and say, "This is what You said. I believe it and I'm claiming an answer to my prayers!"

Genesis 18:14 asks a question, "Is any thing too hard for the Lord?" Jeremiah 32:17 answers that question, ". . .there is nothing too hard for thee."

People doubt in the midst of certain circumstances. They are like the children of Israel when they came to the Red Sea. There were mountains on either side and the thundering chariots of Pharaoh behind and the waters of the sea before them. My, what a circumstance! They trembled. God said, "Fear ye not, stand still, and see the salvation of the Lord" (Exod. 14:13).

You see, when God says something, you can believe it! Many people have doubts because they do not have the Word of God hidden in their hearts when the burdens get heavy. Psalm 55:22 says, "Cast thy burden upon the Lord, and he shall sustain thee." We are to have the Bible hidden in our hearts. When we do not, we doubt.

People have doubts because of sin in their lives. Don't expect to live in sin and have a strong faith at the same time. No Christian is going to have a strong faith with sin in his life simultaneously. Those two things don't go together.

A lot of people have doubts. I have seen those who I believed were saved, but they know more about it than I do. I have seen people I believed were saved as much as I believe that I am saved. Sometimes they will come and say, "I'm not saved but I want to get saved." I would rather they would do that than not come and be lost forever.

Sometimes it is nothing more than sin against God! Doubt comes when Christians have sin in their lives! You are going to have doubt until you can look up to God and claim that you have been cleansed from all of your sins with the precious blood. Doubt comes as a result of sin in a Christian's life.

"Behold, the Lord's hand is not shortened, that it cannot save; neither his ear heavy, that it cannot hear: But your iniquities have separated between you and your God, and your sins have hid his face from you, that he will not hear."—Isa. 59:1, 2.

Doubt comes because of extraordinary circumstances, as I mentioned a moment ago. One of the sweetest things to me is the Lord knew that Thomas was not there the first Sunday night, so He appeared the next Sunday night in order to remove the doubt from Thomas. He can remove yours if you will believe what the Bible says and if your life is clean. You can have the faith that overcomes doubt.

III. THOMAS WAS GUILTY OF THE
SIN OF MELANCHOLY

Thomas was guilty of the sin of melancholy. Every time he opened his mouth, he never said anything encouraging. Did you ever meet anyone like that? Some of you have roommates like that. Some of you may have a life-mate like that. Thomas never said anything encouraging.

There are three great chapters where Thomas is an important and significant character. Chapter 11 of John is one. The news came that Lazarus was sick and that he had died. Jesus said, "Come, let us go to Bethany." Thomas said the strangest thing: "Let us also go, that we may die with him" (vs. 16). He was the kind of fellow who went around to all the doorknobs and hung a funeral wreath on them. He was always possessed with melancholy. Did you ever know anyone like that?

I used to know a dear old lady; everything, everything was negative. You could have a beautiful, sunny day and say, "Pretty weather, isn't it?" She would say, "Yeah, but it won't last."

"Oh, look at the pretty clouds!" She would say, "Yeah, they're weather-breeders, that's what they are."

There are some who say, "You'll never get out of this." Oh, yes you will. There are some who say, "It can't be done here." Yes it can. Thomas was that kind. That is the reason he is known as Thomas the doubter. He was guilty of the sin of melancholy, always with his lip on the ground, always complaining.

"Can I tell you about my operation?" "You don't know how my elbow hurts with arthritis." That was Thomas. In John 14, Jesus speaks sweet, sublime words. He is about to go from this earth. He says, "Let not your heart be troubled: ye believe in God, believe also in me. In my Father's house are many mansions: if it were not so, I would have told you . . . whither I go ye know, and the way ye know." He had been talking about it for a long time. Thomas speaks up: ". . . we know not whither thou goest; and how can we know the way?" (vs. 5). He never did get anything right, never, never!

In John 20, the Lord appeared and the disciples were glad. He walked through an unopened door and a stone wall in His resurrected body. They were the men He knew best! They saw Him and talked with Him. But Thomas said, "I won't believe it unless

I can touch Him and feel Him myself.'' Guilty again of the sin of melancholy. A lot of good people were and are guilty of that.

I think of old Elijah. I will never forget one time as a new Christian when I read the Bible. I started in the Old Testament. When I got to Elijah, I was never so thrilled with anybody in my whole life. Dr. B. R. Lakin said that about the time you get interested in a person, he dies! About the time I got interested in Elijah, something happened to him. I thought of the sixty-three words he prayed and how the Lord opened the heavens and how fire came down and devoured the offering. I thought of old Elijah the prophet. I was a young preacher and I wanted somebody to imitate. When Elijah cut off the heads of four hundred prophets of Baal, I thought, *Go to it, Elijah! God bless you, Elijah!* I was thrilled with Elijah.

One day a woman sent him a message, 'By this time tomorrow, I'm going to cut off your head just like you did my preachers.' He had nerve enough to kill four hundred modernists, chop off their heads down at the brook and let them roll into the water. Now when a woman sends him a message, ''I'm going to see that you get killed, too; see that you get your head cut off,'' it scares him to death. He gathers up his skirts (or robes) and runs into the woods and sits down under a juniper tree.

I read the strangest language. Remember, I am a new convert and a young preacher. Elijah is saying, ''I'm the only one.''

God says, ''No, you're not. There are seven thousand who have not yet bowed their knee to Baal. You're not the only one.'' His circumstances were seven thousand times better than he thought they were!

Did you ever meet a Christian who thought he was the only one? I know one man who thinks he is the only fundamentalist in the world. He would tell you so. I know a man who thinks he is the only preacher on earth who takes a stand. Everybody is weak except him.

Elijah said, "I'm the only one." That is bad enough to begin thinking you are the only one, but he said something else: "I want to be alone; I don't want to see anybody. I don't want to talk to anybody." Finally he said, "I'd just like to die." Elijah came apart at the seams. I said to myself, *What in the world has happened to my prophet who thrilled me so?*

I will tell you. He got possessed with melancholy.

It is a sin for a Christian to have his lip down on the ground like everything is going to wreck and ruin. Listen! You are a child of the King! You are somebody! You are a member of a royal family! God is your Father! The resources of Heaven are yours! You have no business under a juniper tree.

I used to ask—I don't do this much anymore—"How are you doing?" Do not get in the habit of asking that question. I have asked preachers, "How are you getting along?" With a long face they answered, "Well, pretty good under the circumstances." My heart could be revived and I could be thrilled and happy in the Lord, then I see some preacher with a long face and ask, "How are you doing?" "Not so good; under the circumstances," and by now I need a revival. I am down where he is.

That was Thomas. O God, give us Christians who lift people. Give us people whose radiance is contagious. God does not want Christians living under the circumstances!

Jonah was guilty of this. I will never understand Jonah as long as I live. I have read the book of Jonah over and over. I have asked the Lord to help me understand what happened to Jonah. He had a revival where 120,000 adults were saved, besides children. The whole city repented. Then Jonah went out and got under a gourd vine. I have studied commentaries. I have read volumes to see if I could find what happened to Jonah! One commentary said that the gourd vine was a vine that they extracted a substance from to make castor oil. The more I read about Jonah, the more I wish somebody had given him a dose of that! He sat under that gourd vine and pouted and was mad at God—and after one of the greatest victories ever seen in the world. Jonah was guilty of the sin of melancholy.

We have churches full of unhappy people—professing Christians, Sunday school teachers, leaders. They are miserable! Why? Because they are guilty of the sin of doubt and melancholy, just like Thomas was.

IV. THOMAS GAVE A GREAT TESTIMONY OF CHRIST

Thomas gave, I guess, about the greatest testimony that anybody in the New Testament ever gave. I like the testimony of Peter. Jesus said in Caesarea Philippi, "Whom do men say that I am? Whom do you say that I am?" Peter said, "Thou art the Christ, the Son of the living God" (Matt. 16:16).

I like the testimony of Thomas, when the Lord looked right at him and said, "Thomas, here I am. You want to touch Me? Then go ahead. Put your hand in My side. Go ahead. Here it is, Thomas." I do not know whether he felt of Him or not, but I know what he said: "My Lord and my God" (John 20:28). He was never the same after that. He said, "You are not only my Jesus, but You're God!" No greater testimony can human heart give than that made by Thomas: "My Lord and my God!" He not only believed in the deity of Jesus but he believed in His identity with the Father. He accepted the Lordship of Christ.

The next appearance of Jesus to the disciples is the great episode at the Sea of Galilee, recorded in John 21. Thomas was there this time because he had accepted the Lordship of Christ. He was now yielded to Christ.

V. HE CONTINUED WITH THE LORD

I close with something I like about Thomas. The fifth picture of him shows he continued with the Lord. When you get out of the Gospels and into Acts 1, it mentions the eleven—Judas is gone now—and tells what they are doing. They are in an Upper Room in prayer and supplication.

Thomas was a continuing Christian. Give me that kind, those who keep on keeping on. They may be slow, but they get there. I don't like the Christian who, like the runner in the Old Testament runs faster than everybody but, when he gets there, he doesn't know what to say. A fellow who runs not quite as fast will get the message straight and deliver it properly. Give us Christians who continue and are faithful, like Thomas.

On the day of Pentecost Peter stood up with the eleven. While Peter was preaching, there stood old Thomas. He was no doubt saying, "Go to it, Simon Peter!" It is wonderful to find him in the book of Acts, in prayer and fellowship. God had done something in his life! He was a continuing Christian.

"Therefore, my beloved brethren, be ye stedfast, unmoveable, always abounding in the work of the Lord, forasmuch as ye know that your labour is not in vain in the Lord."—I Cor. 15:58.

"And Thomas answered and said unto him, My Lord and my God."—John 20:28.

Chapter IX

Matthew—the Tax-Collector

READ: Matthew 9:1-15.

"And as Jesus passed forth from thence, he saw a man, named Matthew, sitting at the receipt of custom: and he saith unto him, Follow me. And he arose, and followed him."—Matt. 9:9.

The conversion, call, life and ministry of Matthew show that Jesus saves wicked sinners from all walks of life. Matthew was a tax-collector and a very wicked man. In fact, Matthew's life was against the whole plan of God. Rome ruled the world. These people, like Matthew, would buy certain areas from Rome, from which they were to collect taxes. Great portions of that money would go to the publican and tax-collector himself.

The Jews were looking for the kingdom to come; not when Rome would rule the world, but when Israel would own her own possessions and the Lord Jesus would be her King and would rule over the Jews in their native land.

This whole system of Roman rule and taxes and this whole group of tax-collectors and publicans were against the whole Bible, the whole plan of God, the whole future of Israel and the whole Kingship of the Lord Jesus Christ.

Matthew's salvation, call and life show that the Lord saved people from all walks of life. First Timothy 1:15, "This is a faithful saying, and worthy of all acceptation, that Christ Jesus came into the world to save sinners...."

After Jesus had saved Matthew, Matthew said, 'Jesus, I want You to go home with me.' He had invited many other tax-collectors and publicans and sinners. Many notable sinners filled his house.

Jesus was criticized by the Pharisees for going. "Why eateth your Master with publicans and sinners?" Because Jesus wants to save the sinner, He went to Matthew's house.

Jesus made a tremendous statement to these Pharisees: "...for I am not come to call the righteous, but sinners to repentance" (vs. 13). He said in that same house and during that same conversation, "They that be whole need not a physician, but they that are sick" (vs. 12). It is the responsibility of the church to go out and reach the lost from all walks of life.

I said to somebody recently, "It is not always easy to hold up standards. We have standards and codes at this church and we try to present them to our people—standards about dress, appearance and other things. We want to look and act like Christians. But you could come to this church on any given Sunday and you might see somebody in a pair of hot pants or cold pants or most any other kind of pants. I never want it to be any other way, because those people Christians have gone out and won and are bringing to church to be saved.

That is the way it ought to be. I want you to know that the will of God is not that just the righteous, but all sinners be called to repentance. That is why Jesus came and that is why you find Him in the midst of a whole bunch of sinners. We want to win these people, then we will teach them to dress modestly.

I am afraid that in fundamentalism today there are still a lot of Pharisees. These touch not, taste not, smell not kind of people call themselves separated. They are not only separated but they are isolated. They are stagnated. They would not touch a sinner with a ten-foot pole. That is not the will of God for people like you and me! Thank God, in our church you find people coming to be saved from all walks of life.

The conversion, the call, the life of Matthew show that Jesus is "able also to save them to the uttermost that come unto God by him, seeing he ever liveth to make intercession for them" (Heb. 7:25).

It shows also that the past life of a saved person is completely forgiven. No more unlikely man for a disciple you will ever consider in the Bible than Matthew. He had been against these people. His whole life, work and calling had been against Jesus Christ and the Bible. How could he be a disciple? Thank God, that is the miracle of regeneration! The miracle of being a Christian is that God removes all our past life and it is not held against the believer anymore. God remembers it no more.

See two great verses in Isaiah about what God has done with our sins. There are more, but two I have especially chosen. One is Isaiah 53:6, "All we like sheep have gone astray; we have turned every one to his own way; and the Lord hath laid on him the iniquity of us all." He has laid our sins upon Jesus Christ. When a person is saved, the past is blotted out. Then Isaiah 44:22, "I have blotted out, as a thick cloud, thy transgressions, and, as a cloud, thy sins...."

I am so glad the Lord has put my sins behind His back. That means that He is with me and that my sins are not behind my back but behind His back—Isaiah 38:17: "...for thou hast cast all my sins behind thy back."

Before the accuser can ever come to me with my past sins, he has to get around God, because the sins of a Christian are blotted out forever, buried in the depths of the sea and remembered against him no more.

Then the conversion of Matthew shows us that Jesus loves all people. I am glad for this. Now, all people do not love all people. This whole world is torn with strife, racism and troubles of all kinds. The whole human race is not only lost but the human race is against itself. There is enough hatred in the world today to do for all eternity.

God loves people—John 3:16: "For God so loved the world, that he gave his only begotten Son, that whosoever believeth in him should not perish, but have everlasting life." John 13:1: "...having loved his own which were in the world, he loved them unto the end."

"And as Jesus passed forth from thence, he saw a man, named Matthew, sitting at the receipt of custom: and he saith unto him, Follow me. And he arose, and followed him."

I. MATERIAL THINGS GRIPPED MATTHEW

Matthew's whole life was in the grip of materialism. He bought the rights to a certain area. His life consisted not in really living but in making a living at any cost. It didn't matter whom it hurt—widows or children. It didn't matter whom it grieved—God or man. He lived for materialism. His whole life was in bondage to things.

If all you have today is what you can touch with your two hands, see with your two eyes, you are pitifully poor.

I do not know of any subject in the Bible that people know less about than material things. I hear people talk, and I talk to people. I do not know anything that I have heard people speak with ignorance about more than material things.

Look at I Timothy 6:10: "For the love of money is the root of all evil: which while some coveted after, they have erred from the faith, and pierce themselves through with many sorrows."

God said the love of money is the root of all evil. Some folks say, "Everyone who has something is evil." That is not true. My Bible tells me God supplies the needs of His people. My Bible tells me that God loves to give to His own. The Word of God teaches that God honors people who give to Him.

Just because a person has something doesn't mean he is wicked and wrong, that he doesn't love God. A person having something is one thing; that thing having him is another. I have known people who made $75.00 in weekly salary and loved money. Their whole soul shriveled up. Their whole soul was selfish and stingy with God. And their whole life was ruined.

But here is Matthew who says, "I want to get it while I can, and get all I can. I want to get it from the other fellow before he can get it from me." He lived for what he could see, touch and feel, turning out to be a miserable failure.

The Bible tells of many men who loved God and had a lot. Abraham got rich after the Lord called him. Others were rich. God is no enemy to your having something as long as you recognize it as coming from Him and honor Him with it.

Matthew was in the grip of material things. In Matthew 19:22 we read that a young man came running to Jesus. He was rich. Someone has said we may see three pictures of him. Running as a young man to Jesus and going away lost. We hear him one day saying, "I have nowhere to bestow all my goods. I will build greater barns to hold it all." Then we see him again one night when God said, "Thou fool, this night thy soul shall be required of thee." We see him lost in eternal Hell.

This young man comes running to Jesus. The Bible said this rich young ruler had great possessions. He said, "Good Master, what good thing shall I do, that I may have eternal life?" (Matt. 19:16). Jesus told him what to do. Here is one of the saddest things recorded in the Bible. "But when the young man heard that saying, he went away sorrowful: for he had great possessions" (vs. 22). He said, "If being saved means turning over to God not only my soul but all that I have, I am not going to be saved."

I am skeptical of people who say, "I am a Christian" or "I want to be a Christian," who do not want to yield their soul and body, heart and mind to God; who do not yield everything they have, their home, their family and look upon everything they own as being in the hands of God. He went away sorrowful. Money kept him out of Heaven.

You say, "Preacher, this doesn't apply to us." Yes it does. You can have a job tightening screws in the plant and let that job keep you away from God. You can have a menial task in life and let it keep you from being a good Christian.

I know women who worship their homes. They are good housekeepers but sorry Christians. By the way, a good Christian ought to be a good housekeeper. I know men who worship material things more than God. The thing is not so much what you have but what has you. What tells you whether you go to church or not? What tells you whether you can live a separated life or not? What tells you whether you can serve the Lord and give your time to Him or not? What has you today?

Matthew was in the grip of material things.

Matthew 6:33 says, "But seek ye first the kingdom of God, and his righteousness; and all these things shall be added unto you." For thirty-eight years of ministry, I have tried to do just that. Let your life be absorbed in seeking the kingdom of God and getting people saved and honoring the Word of God. I don't believe a Christian has to struggle for his needs when he puts Christ first in his life.

In Luke 16:22, 23 we read of that rich man who died that night: ". . . the rich man also died, and was buried; And in hell he lift up his eyes, being in torments. . . ." That rich man wanted something everyone wants deep down in his heart. But he couldn't get it.

First, he wanted rest of soul. He wanted nearness to God. He said, "Look, there is Abraham. Here is this poor man who died over there in Abraham's bosom. Look where I am. A great gulf separates me from God. I want His nearness." But his money couldn't buy it. He said, "I want mercy." But money cannot buy mercy. Material things do not bring mercy. He wanted water, and the world is full of it—the oceans, the streams, the rivers, the lakes—but not a drop for him. He might have thought, *My material things—I would trade all for a drop of water.* But it was too late. He wanted rest and found none. He wanted the salvation of his brothers but didn't get it.

A lot of Christians have the wrong emphasis in their life; therefore, their families are going to Hell. Once beyond that door of death, it is too late for one to be saved.

Matthew was in the grip of material things and this was ruining his life.

II. HE WAS REJECTED BY SOCIETY

Here is a man, Matthew, absolutely rejected by human society. He was hated because of his position and because of his associates.

The Bible says a lot of things about tax-collectors. They are called publicans. One day Jesus, in trying to win these people, was seen with them and the people asked the question, "Why eateth your Master with publicans and sinners?" (Matt. 9:11). That is the way they were looked upon. Even when Jesus was in contact with them, society criticized Jesus for being near them. That is how rejected they were. Jesus said, "Verily I say unto you, That the publicans and the harlots go into the kingdom of God before you" (Matt. 21:31). These tax-collectors and harlots were looked upon as being the same kind of people—hated and rejected. If people saw them on the streets, they crossed to the other side. They were so rejected by human society that the critics of Jesus said critically of Him, "He is a friend of publicans and sinners."

The Lord saved Matthew, and I am so glad He did. It just thrills me that the Lord loved him. He didn't let these old Pharisees pull Him off. Rather, He said, "I am going to the people who need to be saved, I don't care what they say."

Tax-collectors were completely rejected by human society. Ever since I have been a Christian I have read about Zacchaeus, a politician, a publican and a tax-collector himself. In thinking about the conversion of Zacchaeus, my heart has been thrilled. This fellow—little of stature, little of soul and little of character—was just a little man, with nothing big about him. Jesus was going to pass through Jericho, after Matthew had already been saved. Matthew had had a crowd of tax-collectors, politicians and publicans in his home. Jesus had been there. Perhaps sitting somewhere in that crowd was this short guy named Zacchaeus. He listened and he heard Jesus say, "I came to save folks like you." He said, "They that are whole don't need a physician, only sick people like you." He said, "I didn't come to call the righteous, but sinners to repentance." There sits Zacchaeus.

One day after that, Zacchaeus is in his home town of Jericho, a few hours' walk from Jerusalem. He hears the news that Jesus is coming to Jericho that day. Zacchaeus must have said, "I would like to see Him again." He tried, but taller people stood in front of him and he couldn't get a glimpse of Jesus. So he runs down the street and climbs up in a sycamore tree, thinking, *He is the only one I have ever seen who loved sinners. He is the only one I have ever listened to, talk about mercy and grace, a new hope and a new life for me. Oh, I would like to see Him again!"*

Jesus was walking down the street and Zacchaeus is up in the sycamore tree, with his heart beating loudly. Jesus stopped under that tree. And Jesus knew his name! "Zacchaeus, make haste, and come down; for to day I must abide at thy house" (Luke 19:5).

Here is a man rejected by society who wanted to see Jesus.

Somebody says, "You short little crook, get out of the way!" He would not be denied. "Let me get where I can see Jesus." They reply, "You don't deserve to see Him, you dirty little tax-collector! You cheat people out of their money, you little runt! Get out of the way before I stomp you!" That may have been about what was said.

Jesus didn't look upon him that way. He saw Zacchaeus as a living soul and loved him. Thank God! People can be saved who have been rejected by everybody else.

The alcoholic, rejected, can be saved. The fallen one, rejected by human society, can be saved.

III. HE WAS IN THE GRIP OF THE WORLD

Matthew was in the grip of the world. He lived for the present, in spite of the fact that the Bible says, "A prudent man forseeth the evil, and hideth himself. . ." (Prov. 22:3); in spite of the fact the Bible says, "Boast not thyself of to morrow; for thou knowest not what a day may bring forth" (Prov. 27:1). He lived like he was going to live forever. He excluded God in choosing the world.

I wish I had time to talk about the world. I am not a scholar, just a student of the Bible. I said to you a while ago that I believe folks have more erroneous thinking about material things than about anything else. I am going to say nearly the same thing about what the Bible says about the world. When the Lord is talking about it, most people don't know what the world is. They think of some sin like drinking or immorality. John said, "Love not the world, neither the things that are in the world. If any man love the world, the love of the Father is not in him" (I John 2:15).

What is God talking about when He exhorts us to "love not the world"? He is talking about the whole system, a system ruled over by the prince of the power of the air. It is not just merely this thing or that thing; it is a whole system that took Jesus and nailed

Him to the cross; a system that hates the Bible. God knows we see it in our country. The Bible warns not to speak evil of dignities, and I don't want to violate the Word of God, but the Supreme Court of the United States has dealt, in the last twenty years, more low blows to America than all the communist enemies we have ever had. They took the Bible out of the schools. They forbade prayer in the schools. They are in favor of abortion. They have fought Christianity. They have been against institutions that honor God. That "cosmos" system, that darkened, evil system of rulership that leaves out God—God said not to love that. God never said not to love people. It is not just things. There is so much beauty in this world.

When I was a boy in the country, if somebody had said to me, "How is the ecology down in this part of the country?" I would have thought they were talking about growing some kind of crop! There is a lot of beauty in the world. When I look at the flowers God made, I thank Him for beauty. When I see the sunset splash the gold for miles across the earth, I thank Him for the beauty of this world.

The world is that evil system. Now listen carefully. That system hates a Christian. You say, "How do you know?" I would know it even if I didn't read it in the Bible, because I have felt it. But the Bible says that the world hates a Christian and God says to love not that world, that evil system.

The world was costing Matthew his soul. The Bible says, "For what shall it profit a man, if he shall gain the whole world, and lose his own soul?" (Mark 8:36).

It was the world that cost Lot his family, that world that hates Christians. Every Christian must make a choice. You cannot have the world and Christ at the same time. Paul said, "But God forbid that I should glory, save in the cross of our Lord Jesus Christ, by whom the world is crucified unto me, and I unto the world" (Gal. 6:14).

I will give you an example. One day Pilate saw the surging multitude bring a man before him, a man named Jesus. Pilate had the power in his own hands to choose that Jesus as his own. But no! Pilate was a part of this world system. The Roman government had made him governor and Pilate stands there and thinks in his mind and soul, *If I choose Jesus, I will lose my position of honor in this world system.* So Pilate cried out, "What shall I do then with Jesus which is called Christ?" (Matt. 27:22). Then he takes a basin of water and says what a lot of people say but can't do, "I wash my hands of this whole affair." He washed his hands and the people said, "His blood be on us, and on our children" (Matt. 27:25). It has been all these years. Pilate lost his soul.

The Bible doesn't tell us this but history and tradition do, that later, when he had lost his position, in the country of Switzerland Pilate saw his reflection in the water of Lake Geneva and hated it. He cried out, "Oh, miserable man that chose this world instead of Jesus Christ!" A little while later he plunged his hopeless life into those waters and was drowned.

What are you going to choose, the world or Jesus Christ?

"And as Jesus passed forth from thence, he saw a man, named Matthew, sitting at the receipt of custom: and he saith unto him, Follow me. And he arose, and followed him."

IV. MATTHEW WAS INSTANTANEOUSLY CONVERTED

It has happened to every Christian in this room and it can happen to any person, anywhere, at any time who calls upon Jesus to save him from his sins. Matthew was instantaneously saved.

He sits at his little booth collecting taxes and maybe, amidst the cursing of an unpleasant argument with those who dealt with him, the very next moment that booth is empty. Something has happened to this man. He has been instantaneously converted.

I believe that, in less time than it takes to tell it, the Holy Spirit of God speaks to a lost person's heart and convicts him that he is a sinner who needs to be saved. The very instant one puts faith in the Son of God, that instant he is translated from the kingdom of darkness to the kingdom of light. He is born into the family of God and becomes a new creature in Christ Jesus.

Salvation is not a process. A lot of folks would lead you to believe that to gain salvation you must go through certain exercises which will lead up to the matter of being saved. Not so.

For instance, there are those who say, "When you have learned the catechism, then you become a member of the family of God." No one was ever saved by learning the catechism.

No one was ever saved by good works. Some believe one good work after another finally earns you a place in the kingdom of God. Salvation is not a process. That is why it is impossible for people to be saved by what they call the "Golden Rule," that is, day by day doing unto others as you would have them do unto you.

Salvation is an instantaneous experience in the life of those who believe in Jesus Christ, the Son of God. In a moment, in the twinkling of an eye, Matthew was instantaneously converted.

This demonstrates the magnetic power of Jesus. Oh, the magnetic power of the Son of God! For thirty-eight years I have been trying in my feeble way to lift Him up, knowing that Jesus is magnetic and draws people to Himself.

I will never forget one night in this church when a lady came down the aisle. She made a public profession of her faith in Jesus Christ and following that experience, with the tears of joy streaming down her face, she said to me, "Preacher, when I came in this auditorium tonight, I came, I guess you would say, a curiosity seeker. I never dreamed of such a thing as becoming a Christian." Then she wept with joy as she said, "No one in all this world could be more surprised than I am right now that I have been saved! I didn't plan it but when God spoke to me tonight, in a moment, instantaneously, believing in Him I became a child of God."

I believe one moment a person can be a lost drunkard and the next moment be on his way to Heaven. I believe that one moment a person can be at the very bottom of the gutter and the next moment be seated together in heavenly places in Christ Jesus. That is the instantaneous, miraculous experience called in the Bible the new birth.

Matthew was born again. Matthew was genuinely saved. I can understand why. No doubt he observed Jesus many times. People would come by Matthew, curse him, swear at him, argue with him; but not the Son of God. Jesus would come by and extend His mercy and grace and tell him of His love and His power to forgive him of his sins. One day Matthew's heart was smitten with conviction that he was a sinner and Jesus was the Saviour, and Matthew was born again.

I believe people get saved as a result of observing the right kind of a Christian. More from that than any other way. I think it has as much to do with people being saved, maybe more, than the preaching of the Word of God from a public pulpit. Nothing will keep people from being saved more than Christians not living the way a Christian should live.

Matthew saw in Jesus divinity, righteousness, the Son of God full of mercy, grace and truth, and he trusted Jesus and was instantaneously converted. That can happen to you.

V. HE MADE A GREAT PUBLIC CONFESSION

I want you to see this. Matthew made a public confession of his faith.

Chapter 10 of Romans makes some things very clear about being saved. You are saved by believing in your heart, says Romans 10:9 and 10:

"That if thou shalt confess with thy mouth the Lord Jesus, and shalt believe in thine heart that God hath raised him from the dead, thou shalt be saved. For with the heart man believeth unto righteousness; and with the mouth confession is made unto salvation."

These people who pretend to be Christians but never mention it don't have the salvation spoken of in this Bible. For it says to believe in your heart and confess with your mouth the Lord Jesus.

Matthew made a great public confession of his faith. How did he do it? First, he said to Jesus, "I have numerous friends who are publicans and tax collectors. They are lost people. I have invited them to my home and I want You to come and talk to these people. And I want them to know what has happened to me."

I believe Zacchaeus, of whom we read in Luke 19, was no doubt in that home. He was a publican, a tax-collector, just like Matthew. No doubt he was in that home that day when Jesus talked to all the publicans, tax-collectors and other lost people.

Matthew wanted to make public his confession of faith in Jesus Christ. You too will do that if you are saved. Remember that Jesus said:

"Whosoever therefore shall confess me before men, him will I confess also before my Father which is in heaven. But whosoever shall deny me before men, him will I also deny before my Father which is in heaven."—Matt. 10:32, 33.

You ask, "Does going down an aisle save you from sin?" No! But it indicates to God and man and to all concerned that you want to be saved.

I have had folks ask me, "Do I have to walk down there in front of everybody in order to be saved?"

Well, if you get saved, you won't mind walking down in front of everybody. "Whosoever believeth on him shall not be ashamed" (Rom. 10:11).

I can never get very excited about this kind of salvation where people are silent about it. They don't want to talk about it.

When I asked a man one time if he was a Christian, he answered, "Yes, but I don't want to make any big fuss about it." He doesn't have the kind of Christianity the Bible talks about. I couldn't help talking about what happened in my life thirty-eight years ago, any more than I could help breathing.

A public confession of his faith! He publicly confessed Jesus himself and he wanted others to be saved. One of the first indications that a person is saved is he wants to get somebody else saved. Why do you think so many times in the Bible you read that? The first thing that happened to Andrew after he got saved was, "I want to get Peter saved."

The woman at the well—the first thing that happened to her after she got saved was, "Jesus, pardon me. I want to go back into the city." She comes bringing a whole multitude of new converts. Never been to Bible school, didn't know anything about theology, not a word said about the gift of gab; she who had just been born again wanted others to be saved, too. That ought to be true of every born-again person.

I had a peculiar experience years ago that taught me a great deal about this. Here in the little Castle Inn building, in the early days of this work, was a fellow from North Carolina. This particular fellow was wonderfully saved. He had one of those conversions that just blessed your heart. He accepted the Lord, believed the Scripture, was so happy about it and testified afterwards. He was wonderfully saved. I was so thrilled at it.

The next Sunday I didn't see him, nor the next Sunday. I went to his home a couple of times during that two-week period but couldn't find him. It bothered me to no end. I knew that fellow had been wonderfully saved. There was every indication in the world the Lord had come into his life: now I couldn't even find him. What had happened to this fellow?

About a day or so after I had given up on him, I was walking down the street. I wasn't watching. He came straight toward me, put his hand on my shoulder and kind of pushed me over to the side. I am standing there with my back to the wall, looking at him. It was that same man who had been converted.

I said, "Where in the world have you been?"

He said, "I want to tell you the most wonderful story. After I got saved, I thought about the cousins, aunts and uncles, grandparents, brothers and sisters, nieces and nephews in North Carolina who are lost. When I got saved I wanted to get my relatives saved. I called a preacher down there who had a country church right in the middle of where all my relatives lived." This young man had asked for a special service for his relatives.

This preacher there said, "Who will speak?"

The new convert said, "I would like to. If you will let us have the church, I will be down. I will invite all my relatives."

He said, "Brother Tom, I saw two dozen of them saved in one service! When I got saved, the first thing that gripped my heart was to get my loved ones saved. So I have been in North Carolina two weeks."

That is the way it ought to be. That is what happened to Matthew. He wanted Jesus to come to his house and talk to those people who were like him and needed to be saved.

He made a great public confession of his faith.

VI. HE WAS GREATLY USED OF GOD

Matthew was greatly used of God. He became a disciple. Don't ever take that lightly. Jesus spent a whole night in prayer, then the next day chose twelve, one being Matthew, to be a member of His cabinet. Matthew was greatly used of God.

He went on preaching expeditions. He helped evangelize the whole countryside. He was one of the twelve. God took that old wicked tax-collector and made of him a preacher of the Gospel. That is what God can do for one and all. God mightily used Matthew.

Matthew wrote a particular book. Since the last words of the Old Testament were written, when you come to the last few words of Malachi, there are four hundred years of silence, called the four hundred silent years. No Bible books were written, no audible message came from God for four hundred years.

Then one day God said, "Matthew, I want you to write a book that will tie the Old Testament and New Testament together." That is why fifteen times in the book of Matthew we read, "...that it might be fulfilled." Matthew says that this which is happening is a fulfillment of what was said in the Old Testament would happen.

God used Matthew to write the book of Matthew.

Matthew became a preacher and a soul winner. God is in the business of taking nobodies and making somebodies out of them.

I heard Mel Trotter preach when I was just a young convert. I never will forget how thrilled I was at that big portly fellow. Somebody has said there are no fat preachers. Dwight L. Moody weighed about 250. Mel Trotter had a big institution he could hardly get his hands around!

Mel Trotter was an old drunk in Grand Rapids, Michigan. One day his wife said, "Our baby will die if we can't get some medicine. Go get that medicine. Here is all the money we have."

He took that money and bought another glass of whiskey. In a few hours, the little baby died. Mel Trotter, that old drunken alcoholic, went home, and there was his little baby laid out with beautiful white shoes on her little feet. He came and stole those little shoes off his dead baby to get a few more cents and buy another glass of whiskey.

When I heard Mel Trotter, he was a new man in Christ Jesus.

He had seen people saved by the hundreds in his great mission work. God can take a man from the gutter. He can take a person void of education, like Dwight L. Moody, with about a sixth grade education, and use him mightily. And He can do that same thing yet today. He changes lives. God is looking for somebody He can use.

With a great deal of comfort I often read I Corinthians 1:27, "But God hath chosen the foolish things of the world to confound the wise; and God hath chosen the weak things of the world to confound the things which are mighty." Then verse 29 tells us why: "...that no flesh should glory in his presence."

God likes to take a nobody and make somebody out of him. He is just like a junk dealer; He goes around looking for something, finds it, shines it up and uses it. Then folks say, "It must be God."

That is what happened to Matthew. He was greatly used by God.

VII. WHAT I LEARN FROM MATTHEW'S EXPERIENCE

I learn from this that God may want me to give up something. Matthew had to turn his back on some things. I didn't have that problem when the Lord saved me. When the Lord saved me, I was so proud to get rid of what I got rid of, and I never want it back again. And that was two old stubborn grey mules that nearly wore my brains out. I was so glad to say goodbye to Ada and Ida and leave the farm. It was no trouble to give them up.

But here is Matthew in this great money-making business that was wrong. God said, "Leave it all. Follow Me." From that tax booth he stands and follows Jesus Christ.

The Lord may be saying to somebody, "Will you give up something in order to follow Me and let Me use your life?"

It teaches me that God is looking for full-time representatives. Matthew might have said, like a lot of folks say, "I will tell you what I will do. I will go to church on Sunday. I will tell everybody

I am a Christian." The Lord says, "No, Matthew. I want you to follow Me seven days a week, day and night, twelve months out of the year, and wherever I go. Matthew, it is full time."

That is the kind of Christianity God wants. This business of only Sunday Christianity is sending America to Hell. God wants those who are as good a Christian on Monday morning as they are on Sunday morning. God is looking for full-time representatives who are sold out to go all the way with Him.

I like this because it teaches me that God is no respecter of persons. God can take a man from any walk of life. God cares not about his background; it is his foreground God is interested in. God took Matthew out of all that background and changed his life. He is no respecter of persons.

It teaches me that people who are lost are watching my life. Matthew thought, *Someday, Jesus will get mad. He will lose His temper. Someday I will catch Him in a lie. Or He won't want to pay His honest taxes. Someday I will find a flaw in Him.* But he never did!

A lady got saved. She said, "My life will be different now. No more dance floor, no more beer parlors. My life will be different." Six weeks later her husband said to her, "We have nothing in common anymore. Won't you just this one time go with me tonight? Let's be with our old friends."

She said, "I am dressed. Let's go."

When they got to the door of the beer parlor, the man broke down and began to cry. Leaning over against the wall he said, "O my God! This is the greatest disappointment in my life! I said when you got saved, if she walks straight and true for six weeks, I will know it is real. Oh, if tonight you had just said, 'No, I won't go to that place again!' Now you have destroyed all my hopes."

My friend, somebody watches your life. Remember, you are the only Christian somebody in this world will know anything about. Whether they spend eternity in Heaven or Hell may depend on your life. You say, "It will depend on God and Calvary." No. It will depend on how you live. God is able, but He works through people. It teaches me that people who are lost are watching my life.

It also teaches me that every human being in the world is a candidate for salvation. You never know where you are going to dig up a gem. I have seen them in the strangest places. I have seen them come to the door, little old dirty, ragged, greasy-looking people, and a stench and odor come out of the very door they open. I have seen God save them and I have seen God change them, seen them become like "angels unawares."

I have told the story many times of 230 State Street. I knocked on that door one day at the call of a man who said, "Twelve times at least I have called my church. My sister is sick but nobody will come visit her." When I saw him, I almost said, "I know why nobody will come." There he stood. His clothes were filthy. He had cut off the cuffs of his shirt. They were so filthy even he couldn't stand them anymore. He would sleep in his clothes for two and three months at a time. His hair looked like it had not been combed in a month. A beard of weeks was upon his face.

He led me in a room almost knee deep in debris—paper, magazines, tin cans, and milk cartons—you name it, it was there. He led me over to a hospital bed in the middle of that room where lay a little white form. His sister, a schoolteacher, was dying. I reached and took her little hand in mine, bony and white as chalk, and asked, "Are you saved?"

"No. I am a Methodist but I am not saved. I would love to be." Two weeks later, she went home to be with the Lord. Two weeks later I saw that man again. He looked just like he did before. He didn't go to his own sister's funeral. But he said, "I want what my sister got."

In this room where you are sitting, there is $25,000 of that man's money. At our school, where preachers are being trained and young people are being trained to go around the world taking the Gospel, are thousands of dollars of that man's money. Don't say God cannot work a miracle in a life, for He is looking for somebody He can change and take that tool and use for His glory. Every soul is a candidate for salvation and for Jesus Christ.

I wish we always remembered that. Every man, every woman, every boy, every girl, is a soul Jesus went to Calvary for.

Matthew teaches me that material things do not satisfy the soul. He had all this world's goods he could ever want. He had seen its glitter, had risen to prominence and success in terms of the world, but his heart was hungry. Then one day Jesus said, "Matthew, follow Me."

Do you know what that rich man to whom Jesus said one time, "Thou fool, this night thy soul shall be required of thee," had just got through saying? He had said, "Soul, thou hast much goods laid up for many years. I will build greater barns to hold more grain and corn." Then God in Heaven seemed to look down that night and say, "O man! You cannot feed your soul on corn and wheat. It brings no satisfaction." And in a moment, sitting in his chair, his head drops on a pulseless chest and out into eternity he goes to meet God.

Let me say to you: material things do not satisfy the soul. The comforts of life are enjoyable and God is to be praised for them, but you cannot feed your soul on stocks and bonds.

"Matthew, has all of this brought peace to your heart?" Ten thousand eternal no's he cries; "I want Jesus in my heart."

It teaches me that following Jesus is all that really matters. Hundreds of tax-collectors' names you will never hear because that miracle of grace never happened in their life. One day when Jesus came by and said, "Matthew, follow Me," he arose and followed

Him, and his name will live as long as God lives. Someday, when God hands out the rewards, the glittering crown shall rest upon his redeemed brow and he will praise God forever.

That is all that matters. Following Jesus is the only thing in all this life that really means something.

"And as Jesus passed forth from thence, he saw a man, named Matthew, sitting at the receipt of custom: and he saith unto him, Follow me. And he arose, and followed him."—Matt. 9:9.

Chapter X

James the Less

READ: Mark 15:40-16:1.

"There were also women looking on afar off: among whom was Mary Magdalene, and Mary, the mother of James the less and of Joses, and Salome."—Mark 15:40.

"And when the sabbath was past, Mary Magdalene, and Mary the mother of James, and Salome, had bought sweet spices, that they might come and anoint him."—Mark 16:1.

There is a strange thing about this man who steps out upon the pages of divine inspiration as one of the cabinet members of the Lord Jesus Christ, a member of the apostolate. He is only mentioned eight times in the New Testament. Four of those are in a list of the names of the twelve disciples. Four times he is mentioned in connection with his parents. He is mentioned eight times in the New Testament, and never one time is he quoted.

Not one word that he ever spoke is recorded in the Word of God, not one deed he ever wrought, yet there is no doubt that he wrought deeds. It is thus recorded. He went out preaching because he was a disciple. No doubt miracles were wrought under his ministry because God gave them power to do so. But not one deed he ever performed, not one word he ever spoke is recorded in the Bible. He is called James the less.

James the less is probably a brother to Matthew. There are several sets of brothers in the disciples. There were the brothers Andrew and Peter; also James and John. James the less was a son of Alphaeus. Matthew also was a son of Alphaeus. No doubt James the less and Matthew were brothers. So there were at least three sets of brothers we know of in the apostolate. Six of the twelve were brothers.

I read in Mark 2:14, "And as he passed by, he saw Levi the son of Alphaeus sitting at the receipt of custom, and said unto him, Follow me. And he arose and followed him." So Alphaeus was the father of two of these disciples, a wonderful Christian man himself.

The reason he is called James the less is because he was little of stature. It is not a title given to him, only a description. The word "less" does not begin with a capital letter. It is not a title, only a description of him.

If James lived today, probably his friends would nickname him "Shorty" or "Pee wee." No doubt he was unusually diminutive in his stature, the shortest, the least of all the disciples physically.

We want to distinguish which James this is. There are three men in the New Testament named James. Two are tremendously prominent. There is James, the brother of John. He is always mentioned with John. These two brothers, James and John and Peter—I call the "big three." They are the chief three because the Lord took them with Him sometimes when He took no others: on the Mount of Transfiguration, deeper into the Garden of Gethsemane, and into the room where He raised the twelve-year-old girl who had died. There was this James.

There is another James spoken of by the Lord, a half brother of Jesus. He is the author of the epistle of James.

Then there is James the less, little of stature and little description of him in the Bible. Somebody says, "How are you going to preach about a man if there is not a word recorded that he ever spoke, not one word written about any deed he ever did? How can you preach about somebody of which the Bible says nothing about what he said or about what he did?'' But I notice five tremendous truths about him that I want you to see today.

I. HE HAD GODLY PARENTS

James the less had godly parents. The father of James the less and of Matthew was an outstanding Christian, a leader. ''Alphaeus'' comes from the word ''Alpha'' the first letter of the Greek alphabet. ''Alphaeus'' means ''first,'' ''leader'' or ''chief.''

The father of James the less was a leading Christian man, an outstanding Christian man. James the less had, first of all, a godly father. I could not say too much today about the importance, the need in this country, in churches and in homes, of a godly man to be the head of the home. Alphaeus was the leader of a godly home. No wonder two of his boys were called of Jesus to be disciples. No marvel two of them were called into the ministry. That is the way it should be in every home. ''For the husband is the head of the wife, even as Christ is the head of the church: and he is the saviour of the body'' (Eph. 5:23).

This man also had a godly mother. She is one of the six Marys in the Bible. I have mentioned before my dear old grandfather who lived to be 91 and was saved under my ministry when he was in his early seventies. When he was saved, he began to read the Bible. He read it until his eyes went out. He read through the New Testament 28 times. He read carefully, marking, going over it word by word. He went over the Old Testament a good many times.

He would save up questions to ask me, a lot of which I could not answer. One time he had his big Bible laid out on the dining room table. He said, ''Tom, I can't get these Marys straightened out. Help me distinguish between the Marys in the Bible."

There are six of them mentioned in the New Testament. One is this Mary, a sister of Mary, the mother of Jesus, which would make James the less a first cousin to Jesus Christ as far as His humanity is concerned. "Now there stood by the cross of Jesus his mother, and his mother's sister, Mary the wife of Cleophas . . ." (John 19:25). Though there were two Marys in the same family, they are distinguished by an appellation after their names. Mary the virgin is always distinguished as the mother of Jesus, and this Mary is always mentioned in connection with her sons or family.

This Mary was a godly woman. She learned that Christ was going to Jerusalem to be crucified, to die between two thieves, crowned with thorns, robed in blood for the sins of the world. So all the way from Galilee this wonderful woman, the mother of James the less, follows Jesus down to Jerusalem because she knows He is going to be crucified. She loved Him. She was a godly woman and mother.

Oh, we need in America today godly women. Some godly women have helped keep this nation from going to Hell. I hear so much about "Women's Lib." I would like to see women liberated from cigarettes, cocktails and immodest dress. I am in favor of Women's Lib! I would like to see them liberated from wanting to be the head of the home.

This wonderful godly woman who followed Jesus was the kind of mother James the less had. She was last at the cross according to the Bible. God sent an earthquake and clothed that little hill of Golgotha in a midnight shroud of darkness. Out of that darkness she listened to Him pray, "Father, forgive them; for they know not what they do" (Luke 23:34). She had heard Him say, "O God, don't forsake Me." She had heard Him cry on the cross, "It is finished. I thirst." All of this moved and touched her. She stood gazing afar off, looking fast at the cross.

Not only was she last at the cross, but this godly woman was among the first at the tomb. Luke 24·1 shows that even after He was laid in the tomb, she came to see about His body, to see that it was properly prepared for the burial: last at the cross and first at the tomb.

The secret of the hope of America lies in parents like Alphaeus and Mary. The responsibility for the so-called juvenile delinquency and much of the drug problem today is the fault of mothers and dads. Most do not know where their children are, day or night. Home means nothing. No wonder the youth of America, and in large numbers, are going to Hell. Parents are to blame. That is why I love young people, why I want to see them saved. Most have not had a chance in life.

Here is a man with a godly mother and father.

I read some years ago of a preacher who went to visit one of the ladies of his church who was wanting to do more for the Lord. He said, "Why, sister, you have done much."

"Oh, but I wish I could accomplish something more for Jesus, something lasting for Christ," she replied.

He said, "Now, let's see. You have four sons."

"Yes, four wonderful boys."

"What are their names?"

"Matthew, Mark, Luke and John. I named them all after the first four books of the New Testament."

"Now, let's see. Where is Matthew?" asked the pastor.

"Matthew is in the ministry. He is pastoring a church."

"And where is Mark?"

"Mark has gone to the mission field. God called him to the heathens, to win them to Christ."

"And where is Luke?"

"Luke is an evangelist. He travels up and down the country, telling people about Jesus."

"And where is John?"

"John is also in the ministry. He is a Bible teacher and teaches the Word of God to hundreds of people."

Then the preacher said, "Sister, you say you wish you could do more. Think about what you have done. You have given four sons to full-time ministry."

I stood years ago at a little round stone marker partially covered with green growth in the city of London. That marker bore the name of Susannah Wesley. That marker said, HERE LIES SUSANNA WESLEY, MOTHER OF NINETEEN CHILDREN. On the birthday of every child instead of a cake and celebration, Susannah Wesley spent that day in prayer and fasting, waiting upon God for that particular child. No wonder Charles and John literally set the world on fire. I am saved today because of the work of John and Charles Wesley. I was saved in a Methodist church and God called me to preach there. So I am saved as a result of the life and ministry of a godly woman by the name of Susannah Wesley who put two boys, through prayers and godly living, into the ministry.

James the less had godly parents.

II. HE WAS SELECTED FROM AMONG MANY DISCIPLES

I have often said that I am not a Bible scholar, but I am a Bible student. I read it every day. I try to live in the Word of God. I learn something new all the time. I read Scriptures that I have read scores of times and learn something from them each time. I learned something studying about James the less that never occurred to me before.

Read Luke 6:12, 13:

"And it came to pass in those days, that he went out into a mountain to pray, and continued all night in prayer to God. And when

it was day, he called unto him his disciples: and of them he chose twelve, whom also he named apostles.''

After a night of prayer, He called unto Him all of His disciples, fifty, one hundred—nobody knows how many disciples, but it was a larger group. Of them He chose twelve.

Here is this short man. He must have thought, ''Oh, thank God! Out of this larger group, the Lord has selected me!'' I can say that today. Out of the millions, in His foreknowledge and divine election, He has chosen me and He has chosen you. You are not a Christian just by accident; you are a Christian because you have been elected. Ephesians 1:4 says, ''According as he hath chosen us in him before the foundation of the world....''

You are not predestined to go to Heaven. People get in trouble talking about being elected and predestined to go to Heaven. It is not that. We are elected and predestined to be conformed to the image of His Son. God has ordained that we will wind up being just like Jesus: ''Conformed to the image of his Son.'' That is what Paul is talking about in Ephesians 1:4: ''...that we should be holy and without blame before him in love.''

Thank God, I have been elected! Romans 8:29: ''For whom he did foreknow, he also did predestinate to be conformed to the image of his Son, that he might be the firstborn among many brethren.''

I heard election explained one time by a man who did not know anything about the Bible. You learn most of what you learn from folks who do not know too much about it. Somebody said to him, ''What about this election business?'' He said, ''No problem. There were three who voted. The Devil voted against me; the Lord voted for me; and I untied the vote by voting for myself. The Lord and I have elected me.'' That is just about it. We have been chosen. That is why a Christian ought not hang his head in defeat.

There was this little, short fellow who said, ''The Lord has selected me.'' Jesus, in His providential, all-knowing wisdom, said to the little, short fellow, "I want you.''

I cannot think of any reason in the world why in 1935 He saw a country boy in overalls and tennis shoes in the red-clay hills of north Alabama, came, laid His hand on my life and said, "Tom, I want you.'' It was all grace. I have been elected; so have you. Deuteronomy 7:6: "For thou art an holy people unto the Lord thy God: the Lord thy God hath chosen thee to be a special people unto himself, above all people that are upon the face of the earth.''

III. PHYSICAL APPEARANCE NOT IMPORTANT

Most people go through life literally in opposition to a tremendous verse, I Samuel 16:7: "But the Lord said unto Samuel, Look not on his countenance, or on the height of his stature; because I have refused him: for the Lord seeth not as man seeth; for man looketh on the outward appearance, but the Lord looketh on the heart.''

I think of Saul, the first king of Israel. He stood head and shoulders above all, but died a failure. I think of Samson, the strongest man who ever lived, admired by thousands of people, but he died in disgrace.

It is not the outward appearance. It is what you have inside— character, spirituality. A Christian ought to look the best he can. But God looks on the heart.

I learn by James the less that the Lord can take anybody and use them. The Lord can take a little "shorty" and use him. The Lord can take a runt and make a giant out of him. I learn from James the less that physical appearance is not all important.

IV. HE CONTINUED FAITHFUL TO THE LORD

I believe what distinguishes Christians one from another is

faithfulness. Look at Acts 1:13, "And when they were come in, they went up into an upper room, where abode both Peter, and James, and John, and Andrew, Philip, and Thomas, Bartholomew, and Matthew, James the son of Alphaeus. . . ." Little Shorty is still there.

Jesus had died on the cross, had arisen from the grave, had gone back into the glory, then they meet in the Upper Room, just like Jesus had said do, "Tarry ye in the city of Jerusalem, until ye be endued with power from on high" (Luke 24:49). James said, "I will be exactly where God said a Christian should be." He is up there in that Upper Room waiting for the fulfillment of the promise that the Holy Spirit would come. He was faithful.

You can have all the talent in the world in the work of the Lord. You can be knowledgeable, good looking, and handsome; but if you are not faithful, you will never amount to a thing for God Almighty.

James continued to be faithful. He was the kind of fellow who, when he woke up, looked out and saw five-foot drifts of snow in front of his house, would have said, "There has to be a way. I will get there." James was faithful. The Bible mentioned him at the time the Lord had ascended, so we would know that he just kept on keeping on.

That is one of the greatest attributes. Dr. Bob Jones, Sr., used to say, "The greatest ability is dependability." Three things I like about James. He obeyed the Lord Jesus Christ. When Jesus said, "Tarry ye in the city of Jerusalem, until ye be endued with power from on high," James said, "I will do that."

He was in fellowship with other Christians. Read the list of those who met together and fellowshiped. James was there. That is one of many reasons why the plan of God to evangelize this generation is through the local church and its ministry. God has ordained that a Christian be in fellowship with other Christians. I put no confidence whatsoever in these people who say, "I worship God in the wide open spaces." I worship Him there, too, but I have a church and Christians and a household of faith, and I worship with them. God's Word says, "Not forsaking the assembling of ourselves together..." (Heb. 10:25). If you are not faithful to the house of God, you are not a good Christian.

James was a witness for Jesus. Where do I read that? Twenty-five times in the book of Acts after Pentecost, we read the expression "the apostles," and James was one of them. Twenty-five times you read of their work and their witnessing. James the less was a witness and a soul winner.

V. HE WAS A TRUE DISCIPLE OF JESUS

Lastly, James the less was a true disciple of Jesus. He was called a "disciple" or "apostle." The word "disciple" as used in the New Testament means "learner." From that, one does not learn much about what a disciple is. It is a "learner" in contrast with a "teacher." Disciple means "learner from a teacher." When you read of a disciple, you are reading of someone who embraced, believed and accepted all the teaching of another. A disciple of Jesus was one who said, "I accept the teaching, the truth of Jesus."

There are seven earmarks of a disciple in the Word of God. A disciple must be with Jesus—Mark 3:14: "And he ordained twelve, that they should be with him, and that he might send them forth to preach." The first mark of a disciple of Christ is, he has been with Jesus. He is saved.

Do you know that you are saved today? I do not mean religious; I mean, do you know today that if you died this second you would go to Heaven? Do you know today that you have taken Jesus Christ as your personal Saviour?

Second, a disciple was sent forth by Jesus. The Lord said, "...as my Father hath sent me, even so send I you" (John 20:21).

I have a question in my mind about those who never, never lift a finger to get anybody saved. I will never understand to my dying day how a saved person can be completely oblivious to lost people. A disciple is not only one who has been with Him, but one whom He sends forth.

A disciple obeys His Word—John 8:31: "If ye continue in my word, then are ye my disciples indeed."

A disciple is one whose life is governed by love—John 13:35: "By this shall all men know that ye are my disciples, if ye have love one to another."

A disciple bears fruit—John 15:8: "Herein is my Father glorified, that ye bear much fruit; so shall ye be my disciples."

A disciple is one who forsakes all—many are like the man who said, "Lord, I will follow thee whithersoever thou goest" (Luke 9:57). Jesus said, "Foxes have holes, and birds of the air have nests; but the Son of man hath not where to lay his head" (Luke 9:58). Are you willing to follow Jesus today, no matter what it costs? That is a disciple.

A disciple puts Jesus first. He is not like the would-be disciple who said, "I want to follow You, but suffer me first to go bury my father." Jesus said, "No man, having put his hand to the plough, and looking back, is fit for the kingdom of God" (Luke 9:62).

Are you a disciple of Jesus today? I would like to be known as one by God in Heaven and Jesus, His Son and my Saviour. Wouldn't you?

Chapter XI

Judas Thaddeus—Not Iscariot

READ: John 14:13-26.

"Judas saith unto him, not Iscariot, Lord, how is it that thou wilt manifest thyself unto us, and not unto the world?"—John 14.22.

We only read of this man speaking one time in all of the four Gospels: Matthew, Mark, Luke and John. We do not read a word this one of the twelve spoke but one time, then he asked a question: "Lord, how is it that thou wilt manifest thyself unto us, and not unto the world?" This is the man we are studying about today.

His name is Judas. He is to be distinguished from Judas Iscariot who betrayed the Lord for thirty pieces of silver.

In the twelve, there are three sets who bore the same name. For instance, there are two Jameses. There are two Simons—Simon the zealot and Simon Peter. There are two Judases: Judas Iscariot and this Judas who, after Judas had betrayed Jesus, took his other name, Thaddeus. I am talking to you today about the good man named Judas.

He is quoted as speaking but one time. He is what you might call a background Christian, always standing in the shadows of others, always in the background. He was never up in the place of leadership, or in the forefront, or in great prominence. God seems to reveal to us out of just a little handful of verses in the Bible how wonderful a Christian he was.

He was a truly important man in the times of Jesus. To be one of the twelve was a wonderful position and a tremendous honor. I think of the words of the Apostle Paul when, in great humility, he said, 'I am the chief of sinners' (I Tim. 1:15), and "...who am less than the least of all saints" (Eph. 3:8). In I Corinthians 15:9 he said, "For I am the least of the apostles, that am not meet to be called an apostle, because I persecuted the church of God."

When I read that, I see a person can be the least of all the apostles and still be tremendously important to Jesus. The twelve, called the apostolate, this cabinet of Jesus, were the most important twelve people ever assembled together in the history of the world.

We read of this man's name in Acts 1:13 where the Lord had already ascended and had promised to send the Holy Spirit: "And when they were come in, they went up into an upper room, where abode both Peter, and James, and John, and Andrew, Philip, and Thomas, Bartholomew, and Matthew, James the son of Alphaeus, and Simon Zelotes, and Judas the brother of James." He had already gone back to Heaven. He said to these disciples, "Tarry ye in the city of Jerusalem, until ye be endued with power from on high" (Luke 24:49). One hundred and twenty took Him at His Word and waited in the large Upper Room and in the Temple for the promise of Jesus to be fulfilled.

This man Judas was one of the obedient, prayerful Christians who waited in prayer for the Holy Spirit to come. This is the man we are talking about today, Judas Thaddeus.

I. HIS NAME IS NOT AS IMPORTANT
AS HIS CHARACTER

No one today would name their son Judas because of Judas Iscariot. Some people name a dog or an animal Judas almost in mockery or in fun. Here is a man who bore this name Judas, the same name of another man who would become the most infamous man in history, the man who sold Jesus Christ for the price of a slave.

This man bore the same name, but he overcame its stigma. He made his name mean something. After Judas Iscariot betrayed the Lord, this Judas is called in the Scriptures Thaddeus, which was one of his other names. Thaddeus means "praise" or "praise the Lord." In spite of his name, this man brought honor, glory and praise to the Lord Jesus Christ.

Your name is not as important as your character. Your character is what you are. Your name just designates you as a certain person, so a name is not all that important.

But a name is important. Read Proverbs 22:1, "A good name is rather to be chosen than great riches, and loving favour rather than silver and gold." Notice that God says "a good name." A name is what you make it. Your name is your testimony. A name is what people think of when they think of you. John or Mary or James or Peter—with that name a person or likeness comes to other people's minds, and your name is your testimony. It is what people think of when your name is called.

What comes to the minds and thinking of people when your name is called? Ecclesiastes 7:1 says, "A good name is better than precious ointment; and the day of death than the day of one's birth." What God is saying is that you can put all the precious ointments or perfumes upon your body and make yourself delightful; but better than that is a good name. It says something; it bears testimony for Jesus Christ. Your name is really your testimony of what your life means to people.

For instance, if I call some names this morning, your mind will begin to function about these names. If I call the name of Dwight L. Moody, you think of one of the greatest Bible evangelists who ever walked the face of the earth, a man of whom it is said, "He led a million souls to Jesus Christ and shook this continent for God."

If I mention the name David Livingstone, you think of one who counted not his life dear to himself. He was the first white face many black people ever saw in the heart of Africa. If I mention his name today, you think of a man who died on his knees praying to God to save those black people on that dark, lost continent.

If I mention the name today of George Mueller, you think of a man through whose hands went millions of dollars, none of it sticking to his own hands. All of it was used for little orphan children. It is said that 17,000 orphaned boys and girls were saved in his mission. He sent out great Christians all over the world.

Now, if your name were mentioned today, what would it mean? You know, God has wonderful grace and you can live down a bad name. I may be preaching to someone whose name speaks of failure in life, whose name speaks of sin, of iniquity. But thank God for that marvelous grace about which we sing so often, "Grace that is greater than all our sins." That grace will enable us to live down even a bad name.

Years ago, back in the early days of this country, two boys wanted to steal some sheep. If a person was found guilty of that crime, he was given a horrible punishment. A branding iron was used which had two letters, "ST"—meaning "sheep thief." They would brand it on his brow and he would say with his mouth, "Sheep thief! Sheep thief!" This brand was worn until his dying day. When people saw him with that brand on his forehead, they would say, "That person is a sheep thief." That was their punishment.

These two brothers were found guilty of stealing sheep and were branded. They were so embarrassed and ashamed that one of them said, "I can never live it down. I must leave this community."

But you cannot run from sin. You cannot run from trouble. You cannot run from failure. The only place you can run is to Calvary. The other one said, "I will not run. I can go to God; I can go to the cross; I can ask God to save my life." He did. He lived in that community as a godly Christian until the Lord took him home. Lying in his casket, the people walked by to pay their last respects. Here came a grandfather leading his little grandson by the hand. They looked at this man. Holding Grandfather's hand, the child said, "Grandfather, what are those two letters in his forehead, ST? What are those two letters?"

Knowing how this one lived and knowing how he loved Jesus, the grandfather said, "Grandson, those two letters stand for Saint of God—you know, like St. John and St. Matthew and St. Mark and St. Luke. This man was a wonderful saint."

You see, not only your name, but your whole life can be changed. Your name is not as important as your character.

II. NO MENTION OF HIS CONVERSION OR CALL

I learned from this man, Judas, something else. No mention is ever made of his call. You can remember the call of Andrew, Peter, James and Matthew. You read about how they were on the shores of Galilee. Jesus saw these four fishermen, two sets of brothers, and He said to them, "Follow me," and they followed Him.

You read of Andrew looking over the shoulder of John the Baptist when he beheld Jesus and saying, "Behold the Lamb of God, which taketh away the sin of the world" (John 1:29). Andrew saw Him and Andrew believed. He went back and took Peter with him to see Jesus.

We read of the conversion of Matthew, Philip and others. But we do not read of the conversion or the call of Judas Thaddeus. My friends, this reminds me that there has to be a place and time when you are converted. If you expect to get to Heaven, if you expect to know what it means to have your sins forgiven, you must be sure there was a time and a place when you were saved from sin, when your life was turned about and when you were converted.

Scripture does not mention the time or place of the conversion of this man but we know he was a Christian and that the Lord manifested Himself to him.

I would like to mention that there are lost preachers, even in our city. I have talked to them. I am not speaking in criticism but out of a broken heart. They know nothing about the inspiration of the Bible or the Deity of Jesus, the forgiveness of sins, the second coming of Christ, a home in Heaven or in Hell. They are lost preachers.

A preacher one time was preaching on the subject of conversion. He said, "I have four points to my outline. What is conversion? How is conversion? Why is conversion? When is conversion?" He preached on what it was and got by. He preached on how it was and got by. But when it came to the points of where and when, then he had to ask himself some questions. *Where were you saved? When were you saved? What is the date of your conversion? When did you meet the Lord? Where did you and Jesus get together?* The preacher then said, "There has never been a where or when in my life, but there must be now."

Now I know that people may not always be able to look back and date their conversion. We see saved in this church literally thousands in their early years of childhood. They are saved and they know they are saved and are not worried about that. But the years go forth and the Lord tarries and even if I asked you, "When were you saved? Where were you saved?" you would not be able to say exactly when. The important thing is that you know that there was a place and time when you turned everything over to God.

Paul knew when he was saved and where he was saved. I think it is important to know the time and the place. Read the testimony of the Apostle Paul. Some words in that testimony are tremendously significant. For instance, in Acts 22:6 Paul says, "And it came to pass, that, as I made my journey, and was come nigh unto Damascus about noon, suddenly there shone from heaven a great light round about me."

This was before he was saved, when he went to Damascus to help put Christians to death, as he helped put Stephen to death, a deacon of the church at Jerusalem. He said, "I will tell you where I was saved."

We had a guide point out to us the traditional place, ten miles from Damascus, along the highway, the original place believed down through the centuries where a light from Heaven shown and where Paul was saved, where he met the Lord.

Paul said, "About noon time, about twelve o'clock, and about ten miles out of the city I met the Lord. I know the day, I know when I met Him and where."

Oh, when do you know you met Him? Has there been a time and a place? Consider the matter. What is salvation? What is knowing the Lord? Salvation is accepting Christ as a personal Saviour— John 1:11-13:

"He came unto his own, and his own received him not. But as many as received him, to them gave he power to become the sons of God, even to them that believe on his name: Which were born, not of blood, nor of the will of the flesh, nor of the will of man, but of God."

That is what salvation is! It is not of blood. You do not inherit it. If you have a Christian mother and father, you can still go straight to Hell. If you turn over a new leaf, live the Golden Rule, be a good neighbor, pay your debts, you may not be saved. It is not of man or the will of the flesh; it is the will of God. That is what conversion is. It is because God laid on Christ all your sins: "the Lord hath laid on him the iniquity of us all" (Isa. 53:6).

Where is it? Wherever you meet Christ. You can meet Him under a bush, in the quietness of your bedroom, at the altar of this church, on the highway in an automobile. It is wherever you and Christ come together and through an act of the Holy Spirit of God and by faith you are made one with God.

One time a man, a hobo, was sitting under a railroad trestle. Another came along and sat by him to get out of the rainy weather, and he led this hobo to Christ. Because he was led to Christ under a railroad trestle, the Lord meant much to him. He would witness when he met other hobos and would say to them, "I want you to meet the Lord, but first you have to get under this trestle in order to be saved." He led a lot of people to the Lord, but he always said, "First, you have to get under this trestle. If you don't, you can't be saved." Well, it is all right to get saved under the trestle, but you can be saved anywhere, because the Lord is omnipresent. He is everywhere! He is looking for sinners and can save them anywhere. I will tell you this: when you are saved and have been reborn of God, you should make a public confession of your faith in church and become a part of it.

"Whosoever therefore shall confess me before men, him will I confess also before my Father which is in heaven. But whosoever shall deny me before men, him will I also deny before my Father which is in heaven."—Matt. 10:32, 33.

When is conversion? Well, I know when I was saved, the very week, the month and the year. I know the day and hour. It was the second week of August, August 12, 1935. It was down yonder in the hill country of Alabama where they said there were only two kinds of preachers—the God-called and the educated. If a fellow was educated, it was a pretty good sign to country people that he would not be called of God. The kind of preachers they talked about were the educated and the God-called.

One of these preachers was a Methodist circuit-riding preacher.

He had four churches and held meetings in each one maybe once a month. On the second Sunday in August, 1935, in the providence of God, he stood up in a revival meeting that always started on the second Sunday of August. Why, if a meeting ever started on the third Sunday in August or the last Sunday of July, the Lord would not have blessed it for anything in the world! It had to start the second Sunday of August year to year and never change. He stood up and read a little postcard from an evangelist. The card said, "Due to illness in my family, I cannot come." With great apology, the pastor, Brother Campbell, said, "I am sorry about this, but I will have to do the preaching."

He preached during that revival, and what a revival it was! One morning God spoke to my heart as I heard that big, tall, long, bony preacher with an old-fashioned mustache, that great man, tell about the cross and talk about Jesus and how He died for my sins. That day Jesus walked across the threshold of my heart, a country boy in overalls and tennis shoes. I ran a mile and one quarter skipping and praising the Lord that God had smiled upon me and looked my way! I went back and told my folks that I had been saved.

Do you have a date? Do you know you were saved? Do you know where you were saved? I know. And I know the very spot where one day Jesus and I became one forever.

Is there a time and a place in your life this morning?

III. THADDEUS BELIEVED THE LORD
COULD SAVE AND KEEP

This man Judas believed in the preservation of the saints. Judas or Jude wrote a book in the Bible with just one chapter. But what an important part in this large Book of Scripture is this little book of Jude. He starts it and ends it in the same way.

Think for a moment. Jude had seen a man with the same name,

Judas Iscariot, fail and fall from the apostolate. He was never saved. There is not a more interesting thing about God's sovereignty than to find out why Jesus chose Judas Iscariot. But Jude saw Judas lose his soul and commit suicide. He saw him go to Hell and he wanted to be sure that he was saved.

In the little book of Jude, in verse 1, he said, "Jude, the servant of Jesus Christ, and brother of James, to them that are sanctified by God the Father, and preserved in Jesus Christ, and called." He thanked God that he was preserved.

Call it what you will. Call it that "damnable doctrine of eternal security" if you want to. Or call it what the Bible calls it—"eternal, everlasting life." He wrote one chapter. As he came to the close he said:

"Now unto him that is able to keep you from falling, and to present you faultless before the presence of his glory with exceeding joy, To the only wise God our Saviour, be glory and majesty, dominion and power, both now and ever. Amen."—Vss. 24, 25.

The Lord preserves and He is able to keep us from falling. That blessed truth in the Word of God has never changed. He saves, He keeps. He died to save us, He lives to justify us, to declare us righteous in God's eyes, and He will keep a soul forever. Jude believed that. He believed you were saved forever, not just when you got religion or when you joined a church or got baptized or learned the catechism. You can never be separated. Jude believed neither height nor depth can ever break the ties of salvation. John 5:24 says, "Verily, verily, I say unto you, He that heareth my word, and believeth on him that sent me, hath everlasting life, and shall not come into condemnation; but is passed from death unto life."

A lady and her son were saved one night. The next morning while eating breakfast she said, "Son, do you think it is real? Do you think it is still the same as it was last night?" The worker had given him a little Scripture card that had on it John 5:24. He looked at the card, then said, "Mother, it is still the same. It has not changed." Thank God, it never will! He is my righteousness today. I had nothing but tattered rags and filthy garments, but now I am His!

If I had time I could help you, with the Spirit's help, with these three things so you would never doubt that a Christian is saved forever. First, the nature of His work on the cross. There He spoke seven times. One time He said just one word in the Greek and three in the English: "It is finished" (John 19:30).

Jesus died bearing your sins upon a cross. It is finished! We do not have to keep adding to it every day. He took our sins and bore them in His body—the nature of His work at the cross." . . . but now ONCE in the end of the world [age] hath he appeared to put away sin by the sacrifice of himself" (Heb. 9:26).

The nature of His work at the throne also assures our eternal salvation:

"My little children, these things write I unto you, that ye sin not. And if any man sin, we have an advocate with the Father, Jesus Christ the righteous: And he is the propitiation for our sins: and not for ours only, but also for the sins of the whole world."—I John 2:1, 2.

We have an Advocate at the throne. When I sin, my Saviour represents me. He is my Lawyer, my Go-between, my Advocate, my Mediator. He says, "Father, I know he sinned, but I paid for that one, too"—that one, and that one, and that one from the past, the present and future. "Who was delivered for our offences; and was raised again for our justification" (Rom. 4:25).

Third, there is the nature of our union with Him. The Bible says that we are seated with Him in the heavenlies, or heavenly places. We are down here on earth but "positionally" we are seated in the heavens with Christ today. Colossians 3:3, "For ye are dead, and your life is hid with Christ in God." What is better than being hid with Christ in God?

Dear Dr. Lakin so many times illustrated it this way: "I am hid with Christ in God. Every once in awhile the Lord looks in and says, 'How are you doing, son?' and I reply, 'Just fine.'"

We are hid with Christ in God. I want to take a little time with this. There have been verses that people use in helping someone come to know the Lord Jesus and, in knowing Him, it is determined forever. Some folks do not see it, nor do they believe it. For instance, Jesus in talking with the woman at the well, said, "Whosoever drinketh of this water shall thirst again: But whosoever drinketh of the water that I shall give him shall NEVER thirst" (John 4:13, 14). She goes away, looks back and says, "Jesus, tell me again what You said." He repeats: "You will NEVER thirst."

"All that the Father giveth me shall come to me; and him that cometh to me I will in no wise cast out."—John 6:37.

"I give unto them eternal life; and they shall never perish, neither shall any man pluck them out of my hand. My Father, which gave them me, is greater than all; and no man is able to pluck them out of my Father's hand."—John 10:28, 29.

Never thirst, never lost, never cast out, never perish!

Someone says, "Suppose I were to walk out of His hand?" Then you were never there in the first place. A man in the hand of God knows He is in God's hands, that his sins are forgiven, that his soul is saved, that his name is in the Book of Life. One who says, "I am going back to the hogpen" was never in God's hands in the first place!

Jesus said, "I am the resurrection, and the life: he that believeth in me, though he were dead, yet shall he live: And whosoever liveth and believeth in me shall never die" (John 11:25, 26).

The Bible teaches that one who is saved and knows the Lord will never perish, is never lost, will never die. If that is not eternal, then God is not eternal.

IV. HE BELIEVED IN DEFENDING THE FAITH

Jude believed in the preservation of the saints. He was also a staunch defender of the Faith. In this book of Jude he said, "Beloved, when I gave all dilligence to write unto you of the common salvation, it was needful for me to write unto you, and exhort you that ye should earnestly contend for the faith which was once delivered unto the saints" (vs. 3).

I wish I could stress the importance of defending the Faith like Jude who said, "It was needful for me to write unto you." No Christian is to be contentious, but he is to be a contender. It bears with it the symbol of a wrestler—two men contending one with another. A Christian is to contend for the Faith. Stand for something. That is what we try to do here at Emmanuel Baptist Church. I know we are not perfect but we stand for something. We stand for the Bible. We stand for Jesus. We stand for the Word of God. We stand for salvation.

Jude also mentions three errors people make in the departure of the Faith. First, some have gone "in the way of Cain" (vs. 11), which means no blood. Some today do not believe in the blood of Jesus Christ. They do not believe in His work on the cross because that is a "gory story." They call it "slaughterhouse" religion. That is what Jude said: people "have gone in the way of Cain." No blood!

Look at I Peter 1:18, 19:

"Forasmuch as ye know that ye were not redeemed with corruptible things, as silver and gold, from your vain conversation received by tradition from your fathers; But with the precious blood of Christ, as of a lamb without blemish and without spot."

Now listen carefully. He said, "And ran greedily after the error of Balaam" (Jude 11). Balaam did not believe that a people like Israel could be sinful and be saved. Cain said, "No blood." Balaam said, "There is no such thing as the righteousness of God imputed to people." He thought that because God's people were not perfect that God should curse them. "There is therefore now no condemnation..." (Rom. 8:1).

Then he said they perished in "the gainsaying of Core." He said to Moses, "You are no authority. I have as much right as you. There can be no authority." We have authority today—the Word of God. There is blood—the blood of Jesus. There is justification—the righteousness of Christ. There is authority—the blessed Word of the Lord.

V. JUDAS DESIRED TO KNOW THE LORD

"Judas saith unto him, not Iscariot, Lord, how is it that thou wilt manifest thyself unto us, and not unto the world?" (John 14:22). You say, "How did Jesus do it?" He did not do it bodily. No one of us has ever seen Jesus with the physical eye. "That which was from the beginning, which we have heard, which we have seen with our eyes, which we have looked upon, and our hands have handled, of the Word of life" (I John 1:1).

John said, "I touched Him. I put my head upon His shoulder at the table of the Lord." But we are not going to—not with our physical hands. It is not bodily that He makes Himself known to us. It is not by vision, like when Jacob saw the ladder and angels coming and going from earth to Heaven, a type of Jesus Christ. We are not going to have that vision. Paul touched upon the subject about which Judas inquired, the spiritual manifestation of Jesus, in II Corinthians 5:16, "...yea, though we have known Christ after the flesh, yet now henceforth know we him no more [after the flesh]."

Then how can we know Jesus Christ? Through His Word, through the blessed Book of God. In John 14:8, 9 Jesus promised that people would know Him:

"Philip saith unto him, Lord, shew us the Father, and it sufficeth us. Jesus saith unto him, Have I been so long time with you, and yet hast thou not known me, Philip? he that hath seen me hath seen the Father; and how sayest thou then, Shew us the Father?"

"So then faith cometh by hearing and hearing by the word of God."—Rom. 10:17.

"Being born again, not of corruptible seed, but of incorruptible, by the word of God which liveth and abideth for ever."—I Pet. 1:23.

"Judas saith unto him, not Iscariot, Lord, how is it that thou wilt manifest thyself unto us, and not unto the world?"—John 14:22.

Chapter XII

Simon—the Zealous Christian

READ: Luke 6:12-16.

"...Simon called Zelotes."—Luke 6:15.

The one we want to think about is called Simon Zelotes, which means a zealous Christian, as we shall see later in the message.

Now this brings to mind some wonderful truths. Whenever you study the Word of God, and study about a man, and study about a place, you must remember this is the Word of God. The Word of God is filled with wonderful truths that all God's people need.

When I think about this man, I am reminded of how remarkable it is that God changes a man's life. Now here is a man who needed to have a life-changing experience. That change is described as the new birth, as conversion, as being saved, as coming to know the Lord, as something that has probably happened to most of you in this audience. This man needed to have this happen to him. Every Christian could tell what you were before being saved, and what you are after being saved. In your own evaluation of yourself, you know that a great change has taken place. Paul puts it this way in II Corinthians 5:17, "Therefore if any man be in Christ, he is a new creature: old things are passed away; behold, all things are become new."

That experience will happen to anyone who believes in Jesus

Christ. You can experience a definite change in your life when you trust Jesus Christ. It is a tremendous demonstration of the grace of God. No one can be saved except by God's grace. No one deserves it. No one earns it. No one is worthy of it. "There is none righteous, no, not one." All people are saved on the same basis—of God's grace. Grace is defined as unmerited favor, the undeserved kindness of God, and Simon was saved just this way.

Paul said in I Corinthians 15:10, "But by the grace of God I am what I am...." Every one of us must say that, all who are saved and a member of the family of God.

That was true of Simon Zelotes, Simon the Zealous Christian.

I want you to see four tremendous truths out of the Bible about Simon Zelotes.

I. HE WAS UNDER A CURSE

After searching the Scriptures, we find that Simon was under a curse. The list of the twelve disciples is given three times in the Bible: in Matthew, Mark and Luke. Two of the lists, Matthew and Mark, mentioned that Simon was a Canaanite. Now there is nothing accidental in the Bible. Every jot and tittle is just as God meant it to be. There are no superfluous words, no padding of the pages. When you read something in the Bible, you are reading something the Holy Spirit has thought to be important.

So twice we are reminded that this man was a Canaanite— "Simon the Canaanite," Matthew calls him. "Simon the Canaanite," Mark calls him. He was from the land or the country of Canaan. Some Bible students call him "Simon the Kananite" and say that the appellation does not necessarily mean that he came from Canaan. However, since in both Matthew and Mark he is called "Simon the Canaanite," he must have had some connection with Canaan. But all men are under the curse. The curse of God was upon the land of Canaan. It was even upon a man by the name of Canaan for whom the land was named. Genesis 9 tells of the three sons of Noah from whom the whole human race sprang.

After the Flood there were only four men—Noah, Shem, Ham and Japheth. From Shem comes the Semetic race or the Jews; from Japheth come the great nations such as Russia, Germany and others from that section of the earth's people; but from Canaan, son of Ham, came a country and a people upon whom God pronounced a curse.

After the Flood a strange thing happened. Noah got drunk and his three sons saw him drunken and naked. Seeing the sin of this, two sons were embarrassed. Ham saw him thus and was not embarrassed. He did not see the significance of his father's sin. He merely went and told his other two brothers, but did nothing about it. God said, ''Cursed be Canaan; a servant of servants shall he be unto his brethren'' (Gen. 9:25). God in Heaven said, ''Cursed be this man and his descendants,'' meaning Ham's younger son, Canaan.

This is a picture of all of us. Every one of us is under a curse. Adam and Eve, the federal heads of the human race, fell from fellowship with God and were separated from God and became under a curse. God pronounced the curse upon the whole human race because they had fallen. So every one of us is under a curse. Whatever you say of this man because he was a Canaanite, you must say of every man and woman in this world. They are born to a people under a curse. The Bible says, ''Cursed is every one that continueth not in all things which are written in the book of the law to do them'' (Gal. 3:10).

The word ''Canaan'' means ''the low country.'' Canaan, as it was known in the Bible, was that little strip of country sometimes only a few miles wide, sometimes nearly 200 miles wide. It started just north of Egypt and went northward along the Mediterranean coast 184 miles. It occupied a territory of 11,000 square miles.

When the Lord called the chosen ones, Israel, the elected people, He gave them that land and said, "Drive out the Canaanites; they are under a curse." There were seven nations or sections in that land of Canaan, the people under the curse, the people of the low country and God said, "Drive them out." They were driven out because the curse of God was upon them.

If you are not a Christian, you by all means ought to know it because the destiny of your soul hangs upon, in a sense, the following truth. Every one is born into the world with a sinful nature and is under the condemnation of God, thus needing to be saved—Galatians 3:13: "Christ hath redeemed us from the curse of the law...."

What does that mean? The law said, "...the soul that sinneth, it shall die" (Ezek. 18:4). "Christ hath redeemed us from the curse of the law, being made a curse for us: for it is written, Cursed is every one that hangeth on a tree."

So this man Simon was under a curse just like all are until they get saved. When we get saved, we are not under condemnation, for we are now in Christ Jesus. There is no condemnation in Christ Jesus. In Romans 8:1 we read, "There is therefore now no condemnation to them which are in Christ Jesus, who walk not after the flesh, but after the Spirit." Let me give you an illustration of it right out of the Bible.

Jericho was a part of this land of Canaan. There was a woman in that city described as a harlot because she sold her body to the citizens of Canaan. One day she was met by three spies as they searched out the land for God's people. She hid them. They said to her, "When we come to destroy this city, for destroy it we must because it is under a curse, you can be saved, if, first, you believe this is true and hang a scarlet cord out of your window. When we come to destroy this land and we see that scarlet cord, we will know you and your family are in that home and you will be spared."

Now that is a picture of salvation by blood. When God sees a person under the blood, He spares that person:

"Forasmuch as ye know that ye were not redeemed with corruptible things, as silver and gold, from your vain conversation received by tradition from your fathers; But with the precious blood of Christ, as of a lamb without blemish and without spot."—I Pet. 1:18, 19.

II. SIMON BECAME A ZEALOUS CHRISTIAN

He had enthusiasm, fervor and zeal. That is what "zealous" means. Is the Bible calling Simon a zealous man? Yes. In fact, I found this wonderful thing in studying the man's name—Simon Zelotes, also called Simon the Canaanite. The Hebrew word for zeal is *qana*. The Hebrew word for Canaan is *Kana*. The words for zeal and Canaan are very similar in the Old Testament. The Greek word for zeal is *zelos;* so, whether he is called Simon Zelotes or Simon the Canaanite, the Bible is suggesting that he was zealous.

We read a lot about zeal in the Bible. I am amazed when I look in the Bible, both Old Testament and the New Testament, and see what God has said about His people being a people with a zeal.

For instance, God greatly complimented Phinehas in the Old Testament. When Phinehas saw a man with a Midianitish woman deliberately and flagrantly, in front of all the people of God, commit sins of immorality, Phinehas ran and took a spear and drove it through both of them (Num. 25:6-11). God said in His Word, "... while he was zealous for my sake among them..." (vs. 11). God complimented him and the wrath of God was stayed from the whole assembly of people because of one zealous believer. God help us to have that kind of zeal!

The Bible has so much to say about zeal. I read of Jehu. You have heard the expression, "We speed like Jehu." He drove a chariot fast, so it became a common expression in the country,

"He drives like Jehu." One time Jehu made this statement, "...come with me, and see my zeal for the Lord..." (II Kings 10:16).

What is Jehu talking about? When the Lord appeared to this man and he laid hold by faith on the Lord Himself, he did something that showed he was a zealous Christian. All of his life he was raised in Baalism. His father worshiped Baal; all his people worshiped Baal; and the city worshiped Baal. But when Jehu was called of God, he destroyed the altars of Baal. When the people asked who it was who did this deed, some answered, "Jehu did it." Jehu said, "Come and see my zeal for the Lord."

Both Phinehas and Jehu were zealous about one particular thing and that was being separated unto God. A lot of Christians are hesitant about it. A lot of Christians are afraid they will be called "different." Here are two who were zealous about being separated and letting the whole world know it. I believe a Christian ought to be as zealous about his separation from the world as he is about his preaching, singing, testifying or anything else. So they were zealous Christians.

Jesus was zealous. A prophetic statement about Jesus in Psalm 69:9 reads, "For the zeal of thine house hath eaten me up." Then in the New Testament Jesus looked back, put His hand on that verse and acknowledged that it was prophesied of Him. No doubt this had to do with the time when He went into the house of God and upturned the tables of the moneychangers, took a whip and DROVE them out. He is saying, "The Son of God is zealous for the cause of God."

Christians ought to be zealous for the cause of God. A verse in the Bible has been misused a lot. You Christians have heard about folks having a zeal without knowledge. I suppose most of us have talked about Christians with a zeal and without knowledge. Romans 10:2 says, "For I bear them record that they have a zeal of God, but not according to knowledge." It is not talking about Christians but about unsaved people.

Paul, in this 10th chapter of Romans, said, "Brethren, my heart's desire and prayer to God for Israel is, that they might be saved. For I bear them record that they have a zeal of God, but not according to knowledge."

The Lord doesn't say anything about Christians having a zeal without knowledge. Why? Zeal is of God, even if you don't have all the knowledge. We have enough dead Christianity; we need some Christians with enthusiasm and some zeal for the Lord.

There are three things in the New Testament about which the Bible tells us to be zealous. First is the matter of giving. God says we are to be zealous. In II Corinthians 9:2 the Lord uses the Corinthian church as an example. In talking about giving, He says, "...your zeal hath provoked very many."

Do you know what the Bible says about a Christian's giving? "...let not thy left hand know what thy right hand doeth" (Matt. 6:3). That means, if you give, there is no need to talk about it. I think most Christian's don't. Very few who really gave to the Lord ever did any boasting, if any. But what the Bible is saying is that your zeal of giving hath provoked many. People ought to know that you believe in giving to God. They ought to recognize that, as a Christian, you are zealous about your gifts to the Lord. If it were always that way, then when we got ready to take the offering, we would see the most enthusiastic group of people in the world. "Oh, praise the Lord! It is about time to pass the plate. I just can't wait to honor God with my gifts!"

God wants us Christians to be givers.

Second, a Christian should be zealous of service for the Lord to the saints. "Even so ye, forasmuch as ye are zealous of spiritual gifts, seek that ye may excel to the edifying of the church" (I Cor. 14:12). Paul was zealous about giving and zealous about serving.

He was also zealous in good works: "Who gave himself for us, that he might redeem us from all iniquity, and purify unto himself a peculiar people, zealous of good works" (Titus 2:14). This verse speaks of the fact that we have been redeemed and God has made us a *peculiar* people, not a *popular* people. God never promised that we would be popular. When we find a popular professing Christian, mark it down: he is cutting corners somewhere. God never said a thing in the world about a Christian being popular. Paul was not. Peter was not. And you will not be popular if you are a New Testament Christian. We are a peculiar people zealous of good works.

I would like to illustrate.

Years ago I went up North a few times to deer hunt. A few men in the church like to hunt and they had the audacity to take me with them. In fact, I had a chance to shoot a deer a time or two. I scared one up and he scared me so bad that I just stood and watched him run off. It was a great big buck with a big rack of horns! So, the deer in Michigan were perfectly safe with me around.

On this trip a strange thing happened. There was a big snow in Pontiac and we could hardly get out. I got all outfitted: a big mackinaw coat, boots, socks, ear flaps, the whole "ball of wax." Mrs. Malone knitted me a pair of special mittens. There was one plain mitten and one had a shooting finger. We finally got up North and I had on all this clothing. But we found it to be just as warm as could be in the Upper Peninsula.

We had driven all night, and we hunted the next morning. When noon came we built a fire, made some coffee and we were sitting out in the sage field. We had been awake all night; now all three of us went sound asleep. I woke up when I heard a crackling of fire. I realized that the sage field, with sage as high as your head, was on fire! All three of us jumped up. Our car was parked there and all of our equipment was lying all around. We began to take our big mackinaw coats and beat the ground to put out that fire. When we had finished, I was exhausted. There was not a dry thread on my body. We fought that fire and finally got it put out.

One fellow sat down and started laughing. He said, "Preacher, I want to tell you one thing: if you fight the Devil and serve the Lord with the zeal you demonstrated in putting out that fire, you are really going to be something for the Lord. I never saw anybody more zealous in my life than you were in getting that fire out."

I have often thought that is the way a Christian ought to be— zealous in what he does for God.

I heard an old Methodist preacher preach years ago. I laughed at what he said, but there was a great truth in it. "I like to see Christians do something. Don't just sit there. Do something. If nothing else, fall down." There is some truth in that.

Christians need to do something. The Bible teaches that every Christian ought to be zealous.

III. SIMON AND JUDAS ISCARIOT
WERE PROBABLY FRIENDS

He was probably a friend to Judas Iscariot. I mentioned that the disciples were named in pairs. In Matthew and Mark both were named in pairs: "Simon the Canaanite, and Judas Iscariot, who also betrayed him" (Matt. 10:4). This man is named as a part of a pair with Judas Iscariot. He is named as the eleventh and Judas Iscariot is named as number twelve in all three accounts, in Matthew, Mark and Luke.

You say, "Well, so what?" The Bible says, "A man that hath friends must shew himself friendly: and there is a friend that sticketh closer than a brother" (Prov. 18:24).

Here were two who were probably friends. Jesus sent them out in pairs. Judas Iscariot never changed. He was a friend to him for three and one half years, and Judas never changed. We influence our friends and our friends influence us. This man had no lasting influence on the man to whom he was a companion. "...that no man put a stumbling block or an occasion to fall in his brother's way" (Rom. 14:13).

What kind of a Christian friend are you? What does your life do for those closest to you? I can name some I have been near to in my ministry. I have seen professing Christians lose a loved one forever; I mean let them go to Hell; I mean never win them and see them die and follow them to the grave yard, bury them and say, "I have let my loved one go to Hell." I heard a young man, a professing Christian, say one time right in our church, "God have mercy upon me! I am a Christian but I have let my father go to Hell!" I have never looked into a more distraught and troubled face.

What does your life do to the people closest to you?

IV. HE KNEW PERSONALLY THE LORD
JESUS CHRIST

In chapter 1 of the book of Acts Jesus had died. He had appeared for forty days and had gone back to Heaven. The Holy Spirit is soon to come. In the Upper Room are eleven men in prayer, Simon being one of them. "These all continued with one accord in prayer and supplication..." (vs. 14). He prayed and supplicated to God.

Simon believed when others doubted. He knew what Christian repentance was. He had forsaken the Lord like all the disciples had. In that dark night of His betrayal, Simon had fled with all of them; but, somewhere, he sought and found a place of repentance and restitution. This man was genuinely saved. He was there on the day of Pentecost when the Holy Spirit of God came and filled them. He knew personally the Lord Jesus Christ.

Do you know Him that way? I am not asking you, "Are you a member of a Christian family?" I am not asking you, "Are you a member of a Bible church?" I am asking you: do you know personally the Lord Jesus Christ as your Saviour?

A man once said, when he was trying to lead someone to Christ, "Now do you think I am wrong in being a Christian?"

The other man replied, "Yes, for I don't think there is anything to it."

The Christian said, "Suppose when we get to eternity I do find out I was wrong. There is no God, no Christ, no salvation. But I haven't lost a thing. I have lived a happy life. I had had all the good things that God provides. I have lived the right kind of life. I had the right kind of influence. I have peace in my heart and mind. If I find out I was wrong, I haven't lost anything. But suppose you find out you were wrong."

The unsaved man answered, "If I do, I have lost everything."

Friend, if you are not saved, after one moment in eternity you will be saying, "O my God! I have lost my life and my soul!"

Do you personally know the Lord Jesus Christ? I hope so.

V. SIMON WAS FILLED WITH THE HOLY SPIRIT

He was praying in the Upper Room with the people of God. He was in "one accord in one place" with them when the day of Pentecost came. On that glorious day he was wonderfully filled with the Holy Ghost. "And they were all filled with the Holy Ghost, and began to speak with other tongues [languages], as the Spirit gave them utterance" (Acts 2:4).

All Christians need to be filled with the Holy Spirit in order to have power for service and soul winning. Jesus said, "But ye shall receive power, after that the Holy Ghost is come upon you: and ye shall be witnesses unto me..." (Acts 1:8). Paul exhorted us, "...be filled with the Spirit" (Eph. 5:18).

The power of the church is in being filled with the Spirit. The power for soul winning is in being filled with the Spirit. Oh, to be emptied from all that is not of God, that we might be filled with all the fulness of the Spirit!

"...*Simon called Zelotes.*"—Luke 6:15.

Chapter XIII

Judas Iscariot

"I speak not of you all: I know whom I have chosen: but that the scripture may be fulfilled, He that eateth bread with me hath lifted up his heel against me."—John 13:18.

Several verses in this passage deal with the greatest traitor in all human history. He was not just the greatest traitor of Bible record but the greatest traitor in all history because of whom Judas Iscariot betrayed. He betrayed Jesus Christ. He betrayed God Himself.

Now, why did Jesus choose Judas Iscariot? Nobody will ever be able to give a definite answer as to why Jesus chose one who was not saved and would never be; why He chose one to be in the apostolate who is no doubt in Hell right now. He was called a follower of Jesus and called a disciple. Jesus chose a man who later betrayed Him.

When we study about Judas Iscariot, it is unbelievable all the Bible truth that is brought to focus upon this man. Even the doctrines of the Bible, great truths of the Bible, and the whole great scheme of salvation, is brought into focus when we study about Judas Iscariot.

One thing I notice about him is that he is always mentioned last in the list of disciples and Simon Peter is always mentioned first. I do not believe Peter was mentioned first because of any special reason except his usefulness and fruitfulness and dedication to God. He was probably more useful than the others. He was also a great leader. We always find, without a single exception, Judas Iscariot at the bottom of the list.

Something else about him. Every time Judas is mentioned, it is always quoted that he was a traitor. Every time he is mentioned in the list of the disciples, he is designated as the one who betrayed the Lord Jesus Christ.

You ask, "Preacher, why study about a man who sold Jesus for the price of a slave; one who was never saved; one who did the Lord much harm?" We study him as carefully as we do any of the other disciples. Why was he chosen? Why did Jesus select him? Why was he tolerated for three years or better and Jesus never one time maligned him in an evil way? Why was he tolerated for three long years in the apostolate? Why was he lost? Why do we think he was never saved? We need to study about these things.

I. JUDAS WAS CHOSEN TO SHOW THE DEPRAVITY OF THE HUMAN HEART

Now the selection of Judas shows that the Word of God always exposes the true content of a man's heart. The Bible does not paint up human nature. When someone gets a photograph made, it is touched up, with the shadows removed and sometimes wrinkles, moles, bumps and so forth are covered up. But God never does that in His Word. He reaches up by Holy Scripture and pulls the veneer off of human nature and lets us see it as it really is before Him. God always gives a true picture.

Hebrews 4:12 is a great verse: "For the word of God is quick, and powerful...." Now "quick" means living. You say, "I cut my finger to the quick." The Word of God is living and powerful, "...and sharper than any two-edged sword, piercing even to the dividing asunder of soul and spirit...." The Word of God distinguishes what is soul, flesh, spirit and body. It goes on to say, "...and of the joints and marrow, and is a discerner of the thoughts and intents of the heart." Isaiah 8:20, a verse which means so much to me, says, "...if they speak not according to this word, it is because there is no light in them."

The Word of God throws light upon people, whether they are saved or lost, whether they are right or wrong. The Word of God exposes all these things. "The heart is deceitful above all things, and desperately wicked: who can know it?" (Jer. 17:9). "As it is written, There is none righteous, no, not one" (Rom. 3:10). "For all have sinned, and come short of the glory of God" (Rom. 3:23).

I will deal this morning with one phase of this subject. Why would Jesus choose Judas Iscariot? As I have said, I don't believe any man can fathom the depth and the mystery as to why the Son of God came to save people and to win people. I don't believe anyone can ever fathom the mystery of why God in His great plan, lay His hand upon the life of a black character and sinister figure like this man Judas Iscariot and numbered him in the twelve.

II. JUDAS ISCARIOT WAS CHOSEN TO FULFILL THE SCRIPTURES

I believe there are some explanations that God wants us to see. I believe Jesus chose Judas to fulfill the Scriptures. In verse 18 of the chapter I read to you, Jesus said, "I speak not of you all: I know whom I have chosen...." Jesus knew that hundreds of us would sit here in this auditorium this morning thinking, "Why did Jesus choose Judas Iscariot? Why would He do this?" Jesus said, "I know whom I have chosen: but that the scripture may be fulfilled, He that eateth bread with me hath lifted up his heel against me" (John 13:18). Jesus chose Judas Iscariot that the Scripture might be fulfilled.

Let me say to you, my friends, this Bible is the accurate, unbroken and unbreakable truth of Almighty God. Jesus said, "I have chosen Judas Iscariot that the Scripture might be fulfilled."

It is an amazing and beautiful thing how the Bible shows all the details. It shows in the Old Testament all the intricate details of what would happen in the New Testament regarding Judas Iscariot. The Old Testament said Judas would betray the Son of God. In Psalm 41:9, Judas is mentioned in that Messianic Psalm, that is, it has to do with the Messiah, the coming Messiah, the coming of the Lord Jesus Christ. In that Messianic Psalm, Jesus is speaking, the Messiah yet to come, "Yea, mine own familiar friend." "Friend" here is translated also as "comrade." "...in whom I trusted, which did eat of my bread, hath lifted up his heel against me."

The Scriptures must be fulfilled. Jesus said, "...the scripture cannot be broken" (John 10:35). Whatever this Bible says will come to pass has already come to pass or it must come to pass. When I think of this, I think of the prophetical Scriptures, those having to do with the coming of the Lord Jesus Christ—His coming to earth again, the establishing of His millennial righteous reign over all the world, the coming of the Son of God. They will be fulfilled. The prophecies of the Bible will come to pass.

It looked as if there was no way on earth some fulfillment of some Old Testament Scripture could ever be fulfilled. But they have been! Three-fourths of the Bible is of a prophetical nature, and most of it has already been fulfilled. Only a fool would ever say that the rest of it will not be fulfilled. The Bible predicted the course of history, the course of nations—all laid out in the Word of God so beautifully and without error. These have all come to pass.

Jesus said, "I have chosen Judas Iscariot that the Scripture might be fulfilled." You see, the betrayal of the Lord Jesus by Judas was predicted in the Old Testament. I am going to deal a little later on why he sold Him for thirty pieces of silver. Why thirty? Why not forty-nine? Why not fifty? A definite reason why Judas sold Jesus for thirty pieces of silver. The selling of Jesus was prophesied in the book of Zechariah, next to the last book in the Old Testament. In Zechariah 11:12 we read, "And I said unto them, If ye think good, give me my price; and if not, forbear. So they weighed for my price thirty pieces of silver." Even the selling price of Jesus was prophesied in the Old Testament. Even when Judas Iscariot betrayed the Lord, he sought to repent but went about it wrongly. He never repented really, but took that money and flung it down at the feet of those who gave it to him. They took it and bought a potter's field, where Judas Iscariot rotted in the dust. Even the purchase of the potter's field is prophesied in the Old Testament—Zechariah 11:13: "And the Lord said unto me, Cast it unto the potter: a goodly price that I was prised at of them. And I took the thirty pieces of silver, and cast them to the potter in the house of the Lord." That is where the high priest and Pharisees were who wanted Jesus killed. That is where Judas came and flung the money down at their feet in the house of the Lord. They bought the potter's field hundreds of yards away.

The Scriptures are not only accurate; they are minutely accurate. In every detail, the Scriptures are true. The Scripture that says, "Ye must be born again.... Except a man be born again, he cannot see the kingdom of God" is minutely accurate today.

He chose Judas Iscariot to fulfill the Scriptures. And the whole life of Judas—the betrayal, the selling of Jesus, purchase of the potter's field—the whole thing accurately was portrayed hundreds of years before it ever came to pass, and was fulfilled minutely in the Word of God.

III. HE WAS CHOSEN TO SHOW THE
DANGER OF HYPOCRISY

Jesus chose Judas to show the danger of hypocrisy. I wish I had time to show you how Judas was foreshadowed in the Old Testament; how his whole betrayal was forepictured in the Old Testament.

There was a man by the same name, Judah (or Judas), who was responsible for the selling of Joseph to the Ishmaelite merchants who took him to Egypt. It was Judah who was more responsible for that than any of the other twelve sons. It was foreshadowed when Absalom betrayed even his own father and sought to usurp the kingdom from him. You see, Judas and the betrayal of the Lord is forepictured and foreshadowed even in the Old Testament.

He is chosen to show the danger of hypocrisy. The word "hypocrisy" means "an actor." It is taken from the old-time way of acting. One man played many parts. He just had many faces. He would go backstage and put on one face and play that part, put on another and play that part. They called him a hypocrite because he was a man of many faces.

The matter between a weak Christian and a hypocrite needs to be distinguished. We do not always measure up to what we ought to be. We could be called weak Christians but not hypocrites. Hypocrites deliberately deceive themselves and seek even to deceive God.

See the difference in Peter, for instance. No one ought ever refer to him as a hypocrite. Simon Peter one day said, "No, I am not one of these Galilaeans. No, I do not belong to Jesus." He said it three times. I do not know what was wrong with Peter. I think the reason why he backslid was the same reason why other Christians backslide. He just didn't get his way. In the Garden of Gethsemane he got out his sword, and blood began to fly. He cut off a man's ear, when he meant to cut off his head! He meant business. But Jesus commanded, "Put up your sword, Simon. Don't you know I could call twelve legions of angels from Heaven; but it is for this hour I came into the world. Put up your sword.

To die on the cross is part of the plan of God."

I think Peter was mad that night. I think he said, "Well, if I can't do it my way, then You just go handle it Yourself." I think he got mad and really backslid. But when he heard the cock crow, he remembered Jesus had said, "Peter, before the cock shall crow, you will deny Me three times." He denied Him three times. Jesus told that little rooster, "Now let it go." He crowed in the wee hours of the morning. Now we see Peter bow his head and begin to weep. When he heard the cock crow, he said, "I have failed the Lord, and I want to make it right." He who had denied Him publicly came back and publicly stood for Him on the day of Pentecost and the rest of his life.

There is a difference between a hypocrite and a backslider, or a hypocrite and a weak Christian. If you are saved and look within and see that which dissatisfies and grieves even your own heart, you know you have at the throne an Advocate, even Jesus, the Son of God who keeps you as His own.

"My little children, these things write I unto you, that ye sin not. And if any man sin, we have an advocate with the Father, Jesus Christ the righteous: And he is the propitiation for our sins: and not for ours only, but also for the sins of the whole world." —I John 2:1, 2.

Our state down here may not be perfect but our standing up there is without blemish. He is our Advocate at the throne. Our standing is without a single mark as we stand before our God in Heaven and Jesus Christ.

Judas was a hypocrite, which is shown so vividly in John 12. Everyone should have been so thrilled at what had gone on. Lazarus had been raised from the dead. In that home, in chapter 12, they are having a great supper. Lazarus is being honored, he who had been dead in the grave for four days and the Lord, whose heart had been broken, had brought him to life. Mary was thrilled, for

Lazarus was her brother. Jesus was there. She had a little box of ointment which would cost a person a year's wages to buy—that little alabaster box of perfume or ointment. She had sent for Jesus when sorrow came. He went with her to the grave and brought her brother out of it. She loved Jesus. Taking that little box, she knelt at His feet and broke the alabaster box. The fragrance of the perfume filled the room. She anointed the feet of the Son of God and paid homage to Him.

Then there stood Judas. "Then saith one of his disciples, Judas Iscariot, Simon's son, which should betray him, Why was not this ointment sold for three hundred pence, and given to the poor?" (John 12:4, 5). Judas said, "Why didn't you sell this ointment and give the money to the poor?" We know human nature enough to know people stood around and said, "Well, maybe Judas is right. Here is a man who is missionary-minded. He cares about poor people. There are others in the world besides us. Look at this waste."

Listen to what the Holy Spirit wrote on the pages of the Book of God: "This he said, not that he cared for the poor; but because he was a thief, and had the bag." He carried the bag and he knew that if that perfume were sold and the money put in the bag, he could spend it.

See one thing: God knows the truth. The Spirit of God who wrote this Book says Judas was not a missionary-minded, good man but a thief. He cared not for the poor. God knows the heart. God knows whether a person is saved or not. Judas hid this hypocrisy from the disciples. None knew it. You can't judge people.

Sometimes we have a tendency to say, "Well, I don't see how that person can be saved." We see things in the lives of people and say, "Well, how can a person do that?" The Bible tells us we are not to judge but "by their fruits ye shall know them." I don't think there is anything wrong with being a fruit inspector in spiritual matters. But we cannot know people, so we are not to judge a person. Even the disciples, when Jesus said, "One of you twelve is going to betray Me," wondered who it was.

Simon Peter looked over at John, who always wanted to get close to Jesus. John must have wearied Jesus to death, always wanting to lay his head on Jesus' shoulder. Great big old "son of thunder" John never got over getting saved and he always wanted to love the Lord all the time. Peter said, "John, He said somebody was going to betray Him. Why don't you ask Him who it is since you are the closest to Him."

John said, "Jesus, is it I?"

Peter said, "Lord, is it I?"

Thomas—old, mealy-mouthed, complaining Thomas, said, "Lord, is it I?" I can just hear him now!

James said, "Lord, is it I?"

All wondered, for none knew that Judas was a hypocrite. He fooled everybody but God.

Finally Jesus said, "It is the one with whom I dip the piece of bread into the substance on the table where we are to observe the passover lamb, the passover supper. The one I hand it to is the one." Jesus Himself took the bread, the bread of life, and broke it. He handed it to the blackest, most sinister heart the world has ever known. Judas took it, looked at it and said, "The bread at this supper designates me as the betrayer of the Son of God." He clenched it, no doubt, in his fist, and walked from that beautiful Upper Room, and the Bible said, "He then having received the sop went immediately out: and it was night" (John 13:30). It has been night ever since for Judas. There will never be anything else. He went to Hell because he turned down Jesus Christ. He sold Him and denied Him and betrayed Him.

"I speak not of you all: I know whom I have chosen: but that

the scripture may be fulfilled, He that eateth bread with me hath lifted up his heel against me."

IV. JUDAS CHOSEN TO PROVIDE AN IMPARTIAL WITNESS TO THE DEITY OF THE SON OF GOD

Knowing he had made a mistake, he came back to the Pharisees, the high priests and the religious people—the crowd that killed Jesus! You see religion all over the world, a hodgepodge of every kind of religion there is. Don't forget that religion nailed Jesus to the cross. High priests, Pharisees, scribes, leaders in the things of the Bible—they crucified the Son of God. When Judas knew what he did was wrong, he went back to them and flung that money down and said, "I have sinned in that I have betrayed the innocent blood."

"Then Judas, which had betrayed him, when he saw that he was condemned, repented himself, and brought again the thirty pieces of silver to the chief priests and elders, Saying, I have sinned in that I have betrayed the innocent blood. And they said, What is that to us? see thou to that."—Matt. 27:3, 4.

Remember what they said: "What is that to us? see thou to that." They told him, "You made your bed; now lie in it." That is what the world will say. It allures you, gets you to lower your standards and sell your soul. Do not think you will ever get any sympathy from the world when you want to get up out of the gutter and reconstruct your life. That crowd will say, "You got in there; that is your problem," as they said to Judas. "What is that to us? Who cares how you feel about it? Go your way. See to that yourself."

That is the way it will be at the end of time. People are then going to say, "Oh, what a fool I have been not to trust Jesus! I laughed at those Christians. I said they were a bunch of shallow thinkers and didn't know what they were talking about. I refused

them and turned them down, and I did that to the Lord, too."
In Revelation 6:16, 17 we read:

"And said to the mountains and rocks, Fall on us, and hide us from the face of him that sitteth on the throne, and from the wrath of the Lamb: For the great day of his wrath is come; and who shall be able to stand?"

Judas went to Hell. That is where every person will go who does not know the Lord. That is where I was headed until one day Jesus came to me when I was lost. I am so happy He did. Not only was I lost but heartbroken and disillusioned and living in the Valley of Despondency. I was on the way to Hell. I am so glad I trusted Him! How good God has been to me!

A lady in this church asked my wife and me to go visit a boy in the hospital who had lost one leg. We went. We could see just beneath the sheet, above the knee, the nub of a leg. I went to his bedside and took the hand of this twenty-one-year-old man. I said, "Son, are you a Christian?"

"Yes, I am."

It surprised me. "When were you saved?"

"About three days ago in this hospital."

"You mean somebody led you to the Lord?"

He said, "No. I went up North for the weekend with some of my buddies and we all got drunk. We had a shotgun in the car. While one of my drunken buddies tried to get the shotgun out of the car, it went off and nearly tore off my leg. It took a long time to get me out of the woods and to a hospital. Preacher, I cannot describe the pain I suffered. I thought I would die. I thought of a verse I had heard somewhere in my boyhood, like, 'It is better to go through life with one leg or one hand or one eye, than to enter into hell with two feet.' I cried in the midst of my pain, 'O God, save me!' And the Lord heard. I know I am saved." He glanced down at that nub of a leg and said, "I would gladly give it a thousand times rather than go to Hell.''

May God speak to your hearts today.

V. JUDAS WAS CHOSEN TO SHOW HOW CLOSE ONE CAN GET TO JESUS AND NOT BE SAVED

No one could have been any closer to Jesus in a physical way than Judas Iscariot. He listened to His parables and great sermons. He saw Jesus walk on water and turn the water to wine. He saw the Son of God raise the dead and open the eyes of the blind. He heard all the divine wisdom with which Jesus answered His critics. He broke bread with the Lord at the table. He walked by His side across the dusty miles. He heard Jesus pray many times and he saw the love for the lost in the face of Jesus. He saw Jesus walk among sinful men for over three years, yet he never saw Jesus do wrong in word or deed. But Judas was never saved! From the time Jesus chose the twelve until Judas placed the traitor's kiss upon the brow of Jesus in the Garden of Gethsemane, he was ever so close, yet ever so far from being saved.

Jesus said to the scribe who asked Him which was the greatest commandment, ''Thou art not far from the kingdom of God'' (Mark 12:34). The scribe knew the truth and knew there was only one true and living God. Judas knew these things. He admitted the innocence of Jesus when he said, ''I have sinned in that I have betrayed the INNOCENT blood'' (Matt. 27:4). He knew Jesus was the Son of God, but he never trusted Him as his own personal Saviour. Judas went to Hell in spite of being ever so close to Jesus.

You can hear the Gospel preached plainly and see many others saved, but you yourself must trust Christ for the salvation of your own soul. King Agrippa said to Paul, ''Almost thou persuadest me to be a Christian'' (Acts 26:28). One thief dying close to Jesus on the cross turned to the Son of God for mercy and was saved.

Another dying thief just as close refused to believe and be saved.

Judas Iscariot is probably the greatest example in all human history that you can be ever so close, yet lose your soul, perish in your sins and die and go to Hell. The blessed Bible says, ''For whosoever shall call upon the name of the Lord shall be saved'' (Rom. 10:13).

''I speak not of you all: I know whom I have chosen: but that the scripture may be fulfilled, He that eateth bread with me hath lifted up his heel against me. ''—John 13:18.

___ Chapter XIV ___

Why Peter, James and John?

"And he suffered no man to follow him, save Peter, and James, and John the brother of James."—Mark 5:37.

"And after six days Jesus taketh with him Peter, and James, and John, and leadeth them up into an high mountain apart by themselves: and he was transfigured before them."—Mark 9:2.

"And he taketh with him Peter and James and John, and began to be sore amazed, and to be very heavy; And saith unto them, My soul is exceeding sorrowful unto death: tarry ye here, and watch."—Mark 14:33, 34.

There are some most perplexing and imponderable questions involved in the consideration of Jesus' choice of these three disciples, and the exclusion of others, on certain occasions. Why did Jesus choose only three when He could have chosen more? Why did He choose these three—Peter, James and John? Why did He choose these three on only three occasions during His earthly ministry when He could have included more?

It could be that Jesus was following the principle often taught in the Bible of how a matter should be verified in the minds of the people. The testimony of one man was not enough to cause a man to be put to death under the Mosaic law. The witness of two or three was required. "At the mouth of two witnesses, or three witnesses, shall he that is worthy of death be put to death; but at the mouth of one witness he shall not be put to death'' (Deut. 17:6).

In New Testament times accusations against an elder must never be by only one witness or accuser. Two or three witnesses were required before an accusation would be considered. "Against an elder receive not an accusation, but before two or three witnesses" (I Tim. 5:19).

After the death, resurrection and ascension of Jesus it would be necessary that the proper number of witnesses be able to give testimony to some of the great events which took place in His ministry. These events, the resurrection of a young girl, the transfiguration of the Lord Jesus and His terrible suffering in Gethsemane under the very shadow of the cross, were living demonstrations of some of the greatest truths and doctrines of the Word of God.

The raising of the dead girl not only attested to His power over death but also was prophetic of His own resurrection.

The transfiguration, which was witnessed by the favored three, was certainly one of the most dramatic and beautiful scenes that ever took place on this earth. It was a picture in miniature of the coming kingdom of Christ. Christ is seen in His divine glory. Moses who died and Elijah who did not die are both present on the mountain to give us a picture of the dead being raised and the living being changed and the two being translated together at the coming of the Lord Jesus Christ. Some believe that Peter, James and John, all Jews, represent Israel in the flesh in the coming kingdom. The appearance of Moses confirmed once again that there is life beyond the grave. What a heavenly sight for Peter, James and John to behold!

The third scene that Peter, James and John were allowed to witness was the travail and agony of Gethsemane. They must see the necessity of His death for sinners. They must learn that the greater the sin of man, the greater the agony of his sufferings. They must learn that before the crown comes the cross, and before the glory must come humiliation. In His own sovereign wisdom Jesus provided the biblical number of witnesses to establish forever these great truths.

I. WHY DID JESUS CHOOSE PETER AS ONE OF THE THREE?

We dare not "tread where angels fear to tread" in attempting to determine why Jesus chose Peter, James and John. However, there are some remarkable things about these three men that might be at least a partial answer.

Peter probably gave the clearest declaration of the divinity of Christ that any of the disciples ever gave. Nathanael said, "Rabbi, thou art the Son of God; thou art the King of Israel" (John 1:49). Thomas exclaimed, "My Lord and my God" (John 20:28). However, the great testimony of Peter concerning the identity and deity of Christ is without parallel. It came at the focal point of the earthly ministry of Christ. He is about to announce that He will go to Jerusalem and be crucified by religious leaders. Most Bible students agree that in Matthew 16:21 is recorded the "turning point" of that book: "From that time forth began Jesus to shew unto his disciples, how that he must go unto Jerusalem, and suffer many things of the elders and chief priests and scribes, and be killed, and be raised again the third day."

Notice the expression, "From that time forth." This is a turning point, a peak, a great and critical period in the ministry of Jesus. It is at this time, as recorded in Matthew 16:16, when Simon Peter gives the most complete confession of faith in the deity and identity of the Son of God. "And Simon Peter answered and said, Thou art the Christ, the Son of the living God."

In Peter's ten simple but profound words he used the definite article four times in the original Greek language of the text. His confession of the deity of Christ implies in the use of the word "Christ" that Jesus is the long-awaited Messiah promised in the Old Testament. When he spoke of Jesus as the "Son of the living God," he set Jesus apart from all other mortals; the Living One who was begotten by the Living God who only is the source of all life.

Jesus' response to Peter's declaration of deity was to declare that it was not of "flesh and blood" (human) but divinely revealed by the Father Himself. It came not by human calculation, cognitive intuition or ability but by special revelation of God. No other testimony of the identity of Jesus Christ surpasses this one. So could it be that because of this great confession of faith that Jesus made Peter one of the favored three?

There is something else entirely unique about Peter when compared to the other disciples. He had more to do, humanly speaking, with the founding of the church in its very embryonic stage than any other disciple. The church is built on Christ. It has no human element in its foundation. However, the Scriptures teach that it was the apostles who built upon this foundation, the foundation being Christ:

"Now therefore ye are no more strangers and foreigners, but fellowcitizens with the saints, and of the household of God; And are built upon the foundation of the apostles and prophets, Jesus Christ himself being the chief corner stone."—Eph. 2:19, 20.

Who the prophets were and what they had to do with the foundation of the church is a study which must be dealt with separately. These verses do not teach that the church is founded upon men but men of God were divinely involved in laying the foundation of the church upon Jesus Christ. Jesus taught that the church was built upon Himself, and the Word of God cannot contradict itself. The apostles were not the foundation; they merely laid it. Peter was the prominent one in the laying of this foundation. He preached the Gospel to the Jews on the day of Pentecost and to the Gentiles in the house of Cornelius. This was the first official turning of the Gospel to Gentile people and Peter was God's anointed servant to take it to them. Can it be that the prominent part that Peter would play in laying the foundation of the church moved the Lord to number him among the favored three?

Simon Peter was to suffer for the cause of Christ for some years after the ascension of Christ. In the closing verses of John's Gospel, the Lord told him that he would suffer and die the death of a martyr. The details of the martyrdom are not given in the Scriptures, but Peter knew when the time had come. "Knowing that shortly I must put off this my tabernacle, even as our Lord Jesus shewed me" (II Pet. 1:14). When Peter's suffering came, he could remember and be strengthened by the fact that he had witnessed the greatest suffering ever endured in a human body—the Lord Jesus sweating great drops of blood in the Garden of Gethsemane.

When Peter wrote his two epistles, he wrote of suffering. He used the word "suffer" in one form or another at least sixteen times in the two epistles, the classic passage being that of I Peter 4:16, "Yet if any man suffer as a Christian, let him not be ashamed; but let him glorify God on this behalf." Can it be that because Peter was to suffer so much and write so much to comfort others in suffering that the Lord chose him to be one of the favored three?

II. WHY DID JESUS CHOOSE JAMES
AS ONE OF THE THREE?

James and John were brothers and James is never mentioned apart from John. He was the first to be martyred and John was the last. John outlived all of the disciples and was the last to suffer martyrdom. The record of James' death is recorded in Acts 12:1, 2, "Now about that time Herod the king stretched forth his hands to vex certain of the church. And he killed James the brother of John with the sword."

James and John made a great request of Jesus on one occasion. They had sent their mother to ask of Jesus that her two sons might have the chief seats in the coming kingdom. It is the only recorded event that caused indignation or trouble within the apostolate.

"But Jesus answered and said, Ye know not what ye ask. Are ye able to drink of the cup that I shall drink of, and to be baptized with the baptism that I am baptized with? They say unto him, We are able. And he saith unto them, Ye shall drink indeed of my cup, and be baptized with the baptism that I am baptized with: but to sit on my right hand and on my left, is not mine to give, but it shall be given to them for whom it is prepared of my Father." — Matt. 20:22, 23.

Jesus predicted that James (and John) would drink of His "cup" and experience His "baptism." He was not speaking of water baptism but of suffering and travail. He was speaking of the cup of suffering and the baptism of blood and death.

Jesus used this occasion recorded in Matthew 20:20-28 to teach some of Christianity's greatest truths.

1. He taught that the way to greatness is through service: "But it shall not be so among you: but whosoever will be great among you, let him be your minister" (Matt. 20:26).

Paul was an example of the greatness of serving others: "For though I be free from all men, yet have I made myself servant unto all, that I might gain the more" (I Cor. 9:19).

2. He taught that the way to be a leader was first to be a bond-slave to Jesus and to others: "And whosoever will be chief among

you, let him be your servant'' (Matt. 20:27). The word for servant in this instance is bondslave. In Galatians 5:13 Paul uses the expression, ''by love serve one another.''

The absence of this sweet spirit amongst the family of God is appalling and the lack of this sweet spirit accounts for the lack of blessing and revival in many churches. Humility is an attitude toward God, but true humility manifests itself in a humble spirit toward other believers. ''Likewise, ye younger, submit yourselves unto the elder. Yea, all of you be subject one to another, and be clothed with humility: for God resisteth the proud, and giveth grace to the humble'' (I Pet. 5:5).

3. Jesus taught that the way up is first down and the way to receive is to give: ''Even as the Son of man came not to be ministered unto, but to minister, and to give his life a ransom for many'' (Matt. 20:28). Jesus taught that the blessed one is he who ministers rather than expects to be ministered to.

III. WHY DID JESUS CHOOSE JOHN AS ONE OF THE FAVORED THREE?

It appears that John expressed his love and affection for Jesus more than any of the other disciples.

''Now there was leaning on Jesus' bosom one of his disciples, whom Jesus loved.''—John 13:23.

''Then Peter, turning about, seeth the disciple whom Jesus loved following; which also leaned on his breast at supper, and said, Lord, which is he that betrayeth thee?''—John 21:10.

How outwardly expressive was the love of John for Jesus! Can it be that Jesus rewarded this unashamed affection by including John in the very inner circle of the Lord's relationship?

John was to be given a great and sacred responsibility even as

Jesus was dying on the cross. The mother of Jesus was to be entrusted to the care of John.

"When Jesus therefore saw his mother, and the disciple standing by, whom he loved, he saith unto his mother, Woman, behold thy son! Then saith he to the disciple, Behold thy mother! And from that hour that disciple took her unto his own home."—John 19:26, 27.

Jesus committed the care of His precious mother into the hands of John when He could have chosen some other good man of the apostolate. The omniscient Christ knew that John would outlive all of the others. John was the last of the disciples to die. Jesus knew that because John loved Him so much that he would love and care for His blessed mother until she died.

Jesus took John into the inner circle because He knew that John would write five of the twenty-seven New Testament books. His inspired books furnish an important part of the total revelation of God in His holy Scriptures. The experience at the resurrection of the young girl and the transfiguration taught John much of what he would be inspired to write later. He knew that Jesus was the Son of God, the Resurrection and the Life, the Intercessor at the throne and the coming King. The Gospel of John was written "...that ye might believe that Jesus is the Christ, the Son of God; and that believing ye might have life through his name" (John 20:31).

The first epistle of John was written that we might know that we are saved: "These things have I written unto you that believe on the name of the Son of God; that ye may know that ye have eternal life, and that ye may believe on the name of the Son of God" (I John 5:13).

John wrote the greatest prophetical book in the Bible, the book of the Revelation. Broadly speaking, Revelation was written that we might know that Jesus is coming back again. Almost the closing words of that book speak of His second coming: "He which testifieth these things saith, Surely I come quickly. Amen. Even so, come, Lord Jesus" (Rev. 22:20).

John wrote approximately one-fifth of the New Testament. Can it be that Jesus chose him to the inner circle of three because he would be inspired to write so much of the Word of God?

THREE GREAT LESSONS

1. It is wonderful to be intimate with the Lord Jesus. "Acquaint now thyself with him, and be at peace: thereby good shall come unto thee" (Job 22:21).

2. It is wonderful to be needed by the Lord. "And if any man say aught unto you, ye shall say, The Lord hath need of them, and straightway he shall send them" (Matt. 21:3).

3. It is wonderful to be where God can use you. ". . . I am made all things to all men, that I might by all means save some" (I Cor. 9:22).

For a complete list of books available from the Sword of the Lord, write to Sword of the Lord Publishers, P. O. Box 1099, Murfreesboro, Tennessee 37133.